> Dear Dr. Campbell,
> We spoke on the ph[one] ... about my
> upcoming book. You
> you allow me to use [...]
> were extremely enc[...]
> Thank you so very much.
>   With admiration,
>   Vivian 12-5-22

I'M NOT VEGAN BUT <u>my cousin</u> IS

fill in the blank

Rhymes, Raps and Other Good Stuff About Respecting and Protecting Animals, Our Health and Our Planet

VIVIAN CHINELLI

I'M NOT VEGAN BUT MY COUSIN IS: Rhymes, Raps and Other Good Stuff About Respecting and Protecting Animals, Our Health and Our Planet

by Vivian Chinelli

Copyright © 2022 Vivian Chinelli

First Edition

Published by SAVE A LIFE Publishing

All rights reserved. However, I give you permission to use and distribute any of my rhymes and raps, as long as you don't modify them in any way. I ask that you credit me as follows: Vivian Chinelli, author of "I'M NOT VEGAN BUT MY COUSIN IS: Rhymes, Raps and Other Good Stuff About Respecting and Protecting Animals, Our Health and Our Planet".

Cover design by Jana Rade

Author services by Pedernales Publishing, LLC.
www.pedernalespublishing.com

Library of Congress Control Number: 2022912267

ISBN: Paperback edition   979-8-9865377-2-6
ISBN: Digital edition   979-8-9865377-0-2
ISBN: Hardcover edition   979-8-9865377-1-9

Printed in the United States of America

DISCLAIMER

The information provided in this book is for educational purposes only and does not substitute for professional medical advice.

I DEDICATE THIS BOOK TO YOU!

Why? Because you are clearly a kind-hearted,
open minded and forward-thinking person
who has chosen to explore, or who has already embraced,
the beautiful and compassionate world of veganism.

So, kudos to you for embarking on
or continuing your amazing vegan journey.

I hope my book will become one of your trusted travel companions
and that you'll share it with folks you meet along the way.

TABLE OF CONTENTS

INTRODUCTION 1
   STRANGE TITLE FOR A BOOK, RIGHT? 1
   WHAT EXACTLY IS VEGANISM? 1
   THE BENEFITS OF BEING VEGAN,
   IN A NUTSHELL 2
   WALKING MY TALK 2
   ABOUT MY "RHYMES AND RAPS" 3
   ABOUT THE "OTHER GOOD STUFF" 5
      QUOTES 5
      VIVIANCHINELLI.COM 5

RHYMES AND RAPS 7

ACKNOWLEDGEMENTS 179

APPENDIX:
QUOTATION CONTRIBUTORS AND CREDITS 182

INTRODUCTION

I'm excited for you to get to my rhymes and raps, but before you do, please take a few minutes to read the Introduction. It will give you an idea of who I am, how I became a proud vegan and avid animal rights activist, and why I felt compelled to write this book.

STRANGE TITLE FOR A BOOK, RIGHT?

As soon as I became vegan back in 2017, I started engaging people in conversations about veganism, traditions, choices, and values. I often opened the dialogue by asking if they were vegan or if they knew someone who was. Frequently, the answer to both questions was "No," sometimes followed by "Sorry, I'm in a hurry, but have a nice day."

Since those early years, things have changed dramatically. So many people, to my delight, *are* vegan, and if they aren't, they often answer, "I'm not vegan, but my _____ (fill in the blank) is." And that's how I came up with the name for my book!

Coincidentally (or maybe not), soon after I settled on that title, I spoke with a gal who, you guessed it, shared with me that while *she* wasn't vegan, her **cousin** was! (And as *my* cousin and I always say, "You can't make this stuff up!")

WHAT EXACTLY IS VEGANISM?

Recently, I had a lovely chat with a neighbor at a nearby grocery store. When I asked him if he knew what veganism was, he answered, "It's a diet of only plant-based foods, right?"

While it's true that as a vegan I adhere to a plant-based diet, veganism is much more than a food choice. Here's how The Vegan Society explains it:

"Veganism is a philosophy and way of living which seeks to exclude – as far as is possible and practicable – all forms of exploitation of, and cruelty to, animals for food, clothing, entertainment, testing or any other purpose, and by extension, promotes the development and use of animal-free alternatives for the benefit of animals, humans and the environment. In dietary terms, it denotes the practice of dispensing with all products derived wholly or partly from animals."

For me, this philosophy is simply part of an overarching and guiding moral principle that instructs the way I strive to relate to all Earthlings (human and non-human animals) every day. It's a principle that promotes compassion over cruelty and a respect for all lives.

BENEFITS OF BEING VEGAN, IN A NUTSHELL

With my attention focused on animal rights issues, I didn't realize, until I did a little more research, that being vegan can also contribute positively to my health, the health of our planet, and to the lives of those who go hungry because of the inequities of our present food system. So many beneficial outcomes for the price of a single choice!

WALKING MY TALK

I was a proud and dedicated Kindergarten teacher for 17 years. Out of all of the subjects that I taught, my most important lessons were about compassion, justice, empathy, and respect.

We would often discuss the Golden Rule, *"Treat others as you would like to be treated,"* and what it would feel like to be in the place of another human being or animal in need.

When an insect wandered into our classroom, I used that as a teachable moment. We'd carefully slide our little visitor into a cup and take it outside to a safe place. I would remind my students that every life, even the life of the smallest insect, needed to be respected and protected.

And yet, I didn't think twice about going home after school and eating the leg – the actual leg – of a slaughtered chicken for dinner. At that time, I couldn't see (or didn't want to see) that my choices were at odds with the values I had been teaching. I just wasn't walking my talk.

For over 30 years, my dear friend Hanna had been trying to get me to acknowledge and speak out against the violence in the industries that exploit and abuse animals. I guess I wasn't ready to do that until 2017, when I turned 65.

One day soon after my birthday, Hanna said something to me that changed everything. "Viv, animals are sentient beings, and a sentient being is **NOT** a commodity." I had heard her make that argument before, but for some reason, on that day, her words made perfect sense. I made the decision, then and there, to act like the person I always believed I was at heart – a vegan. I was finally ready to walk my talk.

I can only hope that a line or two in one of my rhymes will resonate with you as Hanna's words did with me. If that happens, it will have made publishing this book worthwhile.

ABOUT MY "RHYMES AND RAPS"

Back in 2020, I attended my first poetry slam, and was hooked! It was exhilarating to watch brave and passionate poets get up in front of total strangers and rhyme about issues that were meaningful to them. I wanted to do the same.

After two weeks of watching others be courageous enough to speak their truths, I finally got up enough nerve to add my name to the following week's line-up. I planned to read one of four rhymes I had written about the plight of captive animals, but then, before the big day arrived, Covid hit, and *Da Poetry Lounge* had to close its doors.

A few days later, I spoke with my friend, Suzanna, who suggested that I add some more rhymes to my original four and then compile

vivianchinelli.com

them into a book. She said that if I wanted to spread the vegan message, publishing a book of my original poems would be a great way to do that. I agreed. To make a long story short, 77 rhymes later, I was able to turn that wild and crazy idea of hers into reality.

So now, I have the pleasure and privilege to share with you 81 original pieces that I hope will inform and inspire you to live your life as a proud and joyful vegan.

As a dedicated animal rights activist, I am committed to shining a light on the painful and disturbing truth about animal exploitation. For that reason, some of my rhymes may be a bit more challenging to read than others. Acknowledging those truths might be hard at first, but in the end, I believe that facing them is necessary and empowering. I'm optimistic that you will see it the same way.

I would also like you to know that my rhymes were written from a place of understanding. As someone who came to veganism late in life, I completely and wholeheartedly understand any *pushback* you might have to making changes, let alone ones that affect you three times a day. But with any *pushback*, there is always the possibility of *pushing through*, and that's what I hope my rhymes will inspire you to do.

I wish we could meet in person and have a one-on-one, heartfelt discussion about the issues I cover in my book. And who knows, maybe one day that will happen. But until that lucky day, I recommend you search the internet for answers to any questions you might have, and initiate conversations with vegans or with others who are as interested in veganism as you are.

> I believe that the more we explore this issue,
> whether we agree or disagree,
> as long as we do it respectfully,
> the easier it will be, eventually,
> to create a world that promotes compassion.
> That is my dream.
> That is my passion!

ABOUT THE "OTHER GOOD STUFF"

QUOTES

I have paired each of my rhymes with one or more powerful and often-times provocative quotes from various sources (both deceased and alive). These activists, authors, educators, philosophers, doctors, and others, beautifully articulate their thoughts about how we treat animals, each other, our health, and planet Earth.

It is an honor to be able to share their perspectives. I feel that their impassioned insights greatly enrich the quality of my work.

(Extended credits for all of my sources are listed in the Appendix.)

VIVIANCHINELLI.COM

When I became vegan, I scoured the internet for ideas on how to reach out and spread the message. It was then that I discovered a group of inspiring vegans and animal rights champions who helped fuel my activism and refine my outreach skills.

I've learned so much by listening to their compelling speeches and watching their captivating conversations with non-vegans.

You can find links to those speeches and conversations on my website at **vivianchinelli.com**. I hope that you, too, will be moved by their passion and commitment to the cause.

And as time goes by, I anticipate meeting many other powerful advocates and role models who will also motivate, inform, and energize me. I'll be sure to link you to their videos, as well.

While visiting my website, check out my growing list of other resources about animals, health, and the environment.

Finally, I encourage you to revisit my website often, as I intend to update you with other good stuff as time goes on.

vivianchinelli.com

Rhymes, Raps and Other Good Stuff about Respecting and Protecting Animals, Our Health and Our Planet

LIFE'S CHOICES	11
INSPIRED	13
INVISIBLE FORCE	15
WHAT ABOUT PROTEIN?	21
DO UNTO MOTHERS	23
ONE, TWO, BUCKLE MY SHOE	25
DOWNSTREAM	27
MANURE	29
I'M NOT VEGAN BUT MY COUSIN IS	31
YOUR TURN	33
IF YOU KNEW	35
BYE-BYE, RAINFOREST	37
GASSY	39
A WARNING FROM YOUR "MEAT"	41
HEALTH INTERTWINED	43
HUMANKIND	45
SLAM, BAM	47
DON'T SELL YOURSELF SHORT	49
GOOD GRIEF!	51
DO UNTO FISH	53
DUPED NO MORE	55
DEFINITELY NO!	57
DO THE MATH	59
IT'S A THING	61
FEEDING THE HUNGRY	63
DO UNTO PIGLETS	65
SCARED	67

PROCRASTINATED	69
THE NEW TALK	71
YOUNG DAD GOES VEGAN	73
FEEDING OUR CHILDREN	75
COGNITIVE DISSONANCE	77
STREET CONVERSATION	79
GOD'S FIRST CHOICE	81
WHAT ABOUT HONEY?	83
FOIE GRAS (fwäh gräh)	85
IN A VEGAN WORLD	87
IN MODERATION	89
OUR CHOICE	91
LITTLE MISS MUFFET	93
A VEGAN TWIST	95
TURKEY TALK	97
ALONE	99
DO UNTO CHICKENS	101
WHAT'S THE DEAL?	103
CIRCLE OF COMPASSION	105
LISTEN UP	107
BEST FRIENDS	109
INTERVIEW WITH FACTORY FARMED ANIMALS	111
IN SHORT	113
AG-GAG	115
PLACES	117
HAPPY ANIMALS	119
HEY DIDDLE DIDDLE	121
A FIVE-YEAR-OLD SPEAKS	123
MARY HAD A LITTLE LAMB	125
BUT I'M VEGETARIAN ALREADY	127
BOYCOTT	129
TO EAT OR NOT TO EAT	131

A FISH SPEAKS	133
CATCH AND RELEASE (A FISH TALE)	135
VEGAN RESTAURANTS	137
PARAKEET PETER	139
ANIMAL DOCS	141
TESTING 1, 2, 3	143
THE LEAPING BUNNY SPEAKS	145
GET ON BOARD	147
BORN TO BE ME	149
BAD BEHAVIOR	151
READY, AIM, TAKE A LIFE	153
HE'LL NEVER STOP	155
BUT WHERE DO I START?	159
THE LEAP	161
CARTOON ANIMALS	163
LIVING IN PEACE	165
YEH, BUT	167
THE DECISION	169
THE RIPPLE EFFECT	171
YOU CAN DO IT!	173
SPREADING THE WORD	175
THESE VEGANS	177

vivianchinelli.com

"Vegan is just pure love. Love for animals, love for the planet and love for yourself."

MISCHA TEMAUL

"Choices are the hinges of destiny."

PYTHAGORAS

LIFE'S CHOICES

The success of your life
is about the choices you make,
the risks that you take and
some luck thrown your way.

Think big or think small.
Retreat or stand tall.
A life with a purpose
or a life thrown away.

Decisions that make you
or break you, forsake you.
You have the choice
to do great things and fly.

Step out of your comfort and
soar with the eagles.
Break out of your boundaries.
Be brave and fly high!

Have faith that you'll find
all the strength that you'll need
to embrace your new vision,
to thrive and succeed.

You'll be in control.
You'll make it work out.
Your choice to go vegan
will be your best choice.
Without a doubt!

vivianchinelli.com

"*Our greatest opportunities for growth lie in whatever we're resisting at the time.*"

EVE ROSENBERG

"*I am no longer accepting the things I cannot change. I am changing the things I cannot accept.*"

ANGELA DAVIS

INSPIRED

I can't require you,
only inspire you.
It's up to you to inquire.
You have a chance
to change the future,
and if you do,
I will admire you!

vivianchinelli.com

"The most effective way to distort reality is to deny it; if we tell ourselves there isn't a problem, then we never have to worry about what to do about it. And the most effective way to deny a reality is to make it invisible."

MELANIE JOY

INVISIBLE FORCE

I hate to be a pest
but I'd like to put you to the test
and ask you why we eat the animals
we choose to ingest.
We do it 'round the world,
north and east, south and west.
It's a straight-up evil system.
Call it messed up, at best.

So now it's time to ask,
"How'd a nice kid like you,
end up eating sliced-up animals
we toss in a stew?"
It's a story hard to hear,
but don't you fear, I'll make it clear.
So let's just get right to the truth
and we will tackle it here.

It started with such loving words
from dad and your mother.
"Be kind to precious animals,
and do unto others
just as you would have others
do unto you. But now
it's time to eat, my dear.
I've made your favorite,
BEEF stew!"

And there's the contradiction.
It's not fiction. It's so true
that a lie was fed to you
so you could do what you do.
Pet the dog, love the cat
but eat the cow or the chick.
That invisible force has kept us in the dark
and therein lies the trick. →

vivianchinelli.com

"To face animal suffering is to face our responsibility in their suffering."

JO-ANNE MCARTHUR

They tricked us into calling
little piglets, bacon. Hell, we
call a cow a hot dog
or a burger and steak, and
they disconnected us
from the truth at the start.
Now we're stuck with all this illness
and disease of the heart.

We hurt these precious creatures.
They deserve a better fate than
being brutalized then slaughtered
all to end up on our plate.
And then we see and eat
what we call "meat"
without a second thought
about a system we bought into,
one that's terribly fraught
with such corruption and disruption
to our very inner core
that craves compassion and respect,
the need for justice and more.

Our government is shrewd
promoting high-risk food.
They get their pockets lined with cash
and it is we who get screwed 'cause
Animal Farms and Big Pharma
have had a hand in the game and
they're destroying our environment
but won't take the blame.

And we don't want to hear it.
We steer clear of it and fear it,
knowing it requires change
so we don't want to go near it. →

vivianchinelli.com

"I have never felt more embarrassed than when I first recognized my role in this circus of inhumanity."

ALEX O'CONNOR

Yet the time has come
to stand up to that force
and make a fuss,
but 'cause we support the system,
it turns out (sadly), that force ...
is **US!!**

"In the next ten years, one of the things you're bound to hear is that animal protein is one of the most toxic nutrients of all that can be considered. Quite simply, the more you substitute plant foods for animal foods, the healthier you are likely to be."

T. COLIN CAMPBELL

"I've found that a person does not need protein from meat to be a successful athlete. In fact, my best year of track competition was the first year I ate a vegan diet."

CARL LEWIS

WHAT ABOUT PROTEIN?

*"I really want to be vegan
but I have a concern or two.
I'm open to thinking 'outside the box.'
So here's a question for you.*

*What about my need for protein?
Tell me, how do I get enough
of iron, omegas, and calcium
and other important stuff?"*

Plants, my friend. They've got it all.
That's where animals get *their* supply.
There are so many ways
you can learn about that
if you're ready to give it a try.

Don't take my word.
Do your research,
as you move to undertake
a decision that will make you proud.
One of the best you'll ever make!

Now let's celebrate with a vegan cake!

Oh, and while doing your research, look into B12.
There are differing thoughts about it.
You can get it from plant foods or supplements,
but make sure that you don't go without it.

vivianchinelli.com

"We are, quite literally, gambling with the future of our planet – for the sake of hamburgers."

PETER SINGER

"You shouldn't be drinking cows' milk for the same reason that if you needed a blood transfusion, I wouldn't give you cow's blood. It's not meant for a human."

DR. MILTON MILLS, MD

"One of the saddest videos I've ever seen is one in which a wailing mama cow is running after the farmer who is stealing her new born calf."

VIVIAN CHINELLI

DO UNTO MOTHERS

I was born last year, as a female calf in an industry so cruel.
I wanted to stay with my mama cow, but alas, I am no fool.
For I know that my body is no longer mine.
My life's in a human's hand.

I'm enslaved to give and give and give,
to satisfy your demand
for milk, that you don't even drink
from your very own mother's breast.
Please don't take the milk that I'd feed to my child,
to feed your addiction to cheese and the rest.

They make a bull ejaculate. Then his fluids are forced into me.
Would you let this happen to your own body?
Please open your eyes and see that you're assaulting my body
without my consent! Don't you see the hypocrisy?

We're exploited, tortured, and then traumatized
when our babies are taken away.
We work for our master year after year
until that fateful day when we drop from sheer exhaustion.
When our bodies cry out "NO MORE!"
Then we're killed for "meat," like our family before us.
What was all of this suffering for?

A bill of goods was sold to you that our lives are yours to steal.
And for what? Some ice cream? Yogurt?
Just five minutes of a meal?
What if this were happening to you and yours?
Tell me how would that make *you* feel?

It's all so sad but you can change it.
Speak up and fight the fight
for all of us who inhabit the earth.
Check your heart, you know it's right.

vivianchinelli.com

"Perhaps one of the most important things you can do for human beings is wean them off an animal-based diet. It hardens the arteries and runs up our health-care costs. The last thing a poor person can afford is a heart attack or cancer or a stroke. And that's all linked to a meat-based diet. I think animal liberation is human liberation."

INGRID NEWKIRK

ONE, TWO, BUCKLE MY SHOE
(Another Mother Goose Nursery Rhyme Goes Vegan)

ONE, TWO ... I've got good news for you!

THREE, FOUR ... Lots of choices galore!

SIX, FIVE ... Eat plant-based and thrive!

SEVEN, EIGHT ... It'll make you look great!

NINE, TEN ... And you'll feel fab. **AMEN**!

vivianchinelli.com

"The Earth will not continue to offer its harvest, except with faithful stewardship. We cannot say we love the land and then take steps to destroy it for use by future generations."

POPE JOHN PAUL II

"We don't inherit the earth from our ancestors; we borrow it from our children."

NATIVE AMERICAN PROVERB

DOWNSTREAM

Where does the cow, pig, and chicken poop go?
Sometimes it flows downstream.
It's a harsh reality for those living near.
Not meant to be a funny meme.

100 and 50 gallons of water,
each day for **each cow**, not to drink,
but to wash down the floors filled with antibiotics
and hormones and poop and the stink.

When the waste leaks out to the fields and the water,
it kills everything around,
infecting the powerless who can't fight back,
who try hard just to stand their ground.

A direct attack on public health
against those folks who might not have the wealth
to fight these farms and their poison pollution.
It's time to turn to a vegan solution.

We know what's happening but we won't say a word
until there comes a day, when the poop is flowing
into our backyards.
At which point we'll stand up and say,
"STOP THIS GREAT INJUSTICE!"

We'll each march and hold up a sign.
We'll finally gather and protest together
when it starts to affect yours and mine.

Don't wait for that day when our own kids might suffer.
When it gets to that point turning back will be tougher.

Be vegan and end this madness at last.
Please think of the future and let's move past the past.

vivianchinelli.com

"We have forgotten how to be good guests, how to walk lightly on the earth as its other creatures do."

BARBARA WARD

"It's not a requirement to eat animals; we just choose to do it, so it becomes a moral choice and one that is having a huge impact on the planet, using up resources and destroying the biosphere."

JAMES CAMERON

MANURE

Animal farms.
Manure.
Turning lakes into a sewer, making
locals sick, polluting streams and
robbing them of their future dreams.

Vegans have some sound solutions.
Start a kindness revolution and
ditch destructive institutions.

Because pollution anywhere
will affect our planet everywhere.
So ... BEWARE!

"No one is too small to make a difference, everyone can do something. If everyone did something, then huge differences can happen."

GRETA THUNBERG

I'M NOT VEGAN BUT MY COUSIN IS

"My cousin is vegan."

Great! But what about you?

*"I want to, yet I'm scared.
It seems hard to pursue."*

If your cousin can do it,
I know you can, too.

(The following week …)

*"You were right!
Oh my goodness, what you said is **so true**!
So I changed my mindset.
It was a great thing to do.*

*Now instead of one vegan in my family,
there are two!*

Thanks to you!"

vivianchinelli.com

"To avoid causing terror to living beings, let the disciple refrain from eating meat."

THE BUDDHA DHAMMAPADA

"The question is not, 'Can they reason?' nor, 'Can they talk?' But rather, 'Can they suffer?'"

JEREMY BENTHAM

YOUR TURN

Remember a time you were suffering
and your pain was just too much to bear?
Not fair!

How you wished that someone would help you?
How you hoped that someone would care?

Well, the animals we exploit each day,
their pain is also too much to bear.
Not fair!

Now it's your chance to help those
who can't help themselves.
Now is your chance to step up and care.

Think of all the suffering you could allay
by choosing to be vegan and leading the way.

Be bold, be strong, and save the day!
And stand up against all this suffering!

vivianchinelli.com

"The domestic farm animals we breed for food are individuals, each with his or her own personality, each knowing emotions such as contentment, distress and fear; each feeling pain. They are far more intelligent than most people understand. They deserve our respect. And they need help. Who will plead for them if we are silent?"

DR. JANE GOODALL

IF YOU KNEW

Why do vegans seem
"preachy" and "extreme?"

It's because in their dreams
they hear the screams
or see the streams of videos
on the internet
of a mama cow being brutalized
and traumatized before their eyes.

Her piercing cries that
are masked by lies that say
the mama cow is happy.

It's hard to sit back
and not spread the word.
Make it heard.
So that everybody knows
the reality, EXPOSED!

So until we're open to learning the facts,
it might seem to us like they overreact.

But the truth is,
if we knew
what they knew,
we might be "preachy," too.

vivianchinelli.com

"Imagine a man without lungs. Imagine earth without the Amazon rainforest."

VINITA KINRA

"A nation that destroys its soils destroys itself. Forests are the lungs of our land, purifying the air and giving fresh strength to our people."

PRESIDENT FRANKLIN D. ROOSEVELT

BYE-BYE, RAINFOREST

We're burning down the Amazon
(the forest, not the store)!
Don't you care that our dirty air
won't be absorbed as well as before?

We're burning it down
so that cows can graze
on its two million miles of land.
Is this what we want for our kids?
I'm sure, that this isn't
what we had planned.

I know that saving the Amazon
might seem like an uphill battle.
But we've got to start now,
before it's too late.
Let's agree to stop raising cattle.

'Cause if we don't …

we lose in the end
and Big Business wins out.
That is something that
we must consider.

Unless we don't care,
and are willing to sell
our kids' future
to the rich, highest bidder.

vivianchinelli.com

"It's not my fault. It's yours. I naturally emit methane from both ends and always will. The real problem is the sheer number of us cows that you've put on the planet just to make your burgers. A billion cows, at least. That's a lot of methane.

You're putting us in an impossible situation. If you weren't intensively farming us animals, forcing us to over-graze and destroy plant life, the saved vegetation would sequester carbon dioxide from the atmosphere, re-wild the planet and reverse climate change. Animal agriculture is the cow in the room; it's time to address it. Now."

VEGA THE COW

GASSY

Methane gases,
a burp and a fart.

Now that's a good place
for your research to start.

The animals we breed
affect the air that we need.

So I plead that you
watch,
listen,
think,
and
yes, read!

"*Foodborne: Each year, 1 in 6 Americans get sick from eating contaminated food. Eating or drinking something unsafe, such as unpasteurized (raw) milk, undercooked meat or eggs, or raw fruits and vegetables that are contaminated with feces from an infected animal. Contaminated food can cause illness in people and animals, including pets.*"

CENTER FOR DISEASE CONTROL AND
PREVENTION, ARTICLE "ZOONOTIC DISEASES"

A WARNING FROM YOUR "MEAT"

Most Zoonotic viruses
can spread from "meat" to you.
So eating me may not be
such a real smart thing to do.

There's Mad Cow, Sars, and Covid,
just to name a few.
And let's not leave out Avian,
that really nasty flu.

One day you might get sick from me,
spreading germs from an animal farm, uh!
That's what some might call payback
while some others call it karma.

In either case, consider this,
the choices that you make
might turn and bite you in the ***.

Be vegan, for heaven's sake!

vivianchinelli.com

"We are part of nature – when we protect nature, we are nature protecting itself."

GRETA THUNBERG

"To me, it is deeply moving that the same food choices that give us the best chance to eliminate world hunger are also those that take the least toll on the environment, contribute the most to our long-term health, are the safest, and are also, far and away, the most compassionate towards our fellow creatures."

JOHN ROBBINS

HEALTH INTERTWINED

If you study the balance of nature,
I'm sure that you're bound to find
that our health
and the health of the animals and earth
are most definitely, intertwined.

vivianchinelli.com

"You cannot do a kindness too soon, for you never know how soon it will be too late."

RALPH WALDO EMERSON

"... but human beings, at our best, are so inventive and creative and ingenious and I think that when we use love and compassion as our guiding principles, we can create, develop and implement systems of change that are beneficial to all sentient beings and to the environment.

JOAQUIN PHOENIX

"I am in favor of animal rights as well as human rights. That is the way of a whole human being."

PRESIDENT ABRAHAM LINCOLN

HUMANKIND

Attention!
Did I mention that humankind
needs an intervention?

If we don't voluntarily change our course,
it'll happen by force
and we'll be the source
of a system that's failed
and completely derailed.
So out of wack.
No turning back!

A paradigm shift is what we need, with speed,
to end our unquenchable greed.
(Just dropping a seed.)
I must intercede and plead
that we take the lead
to put the "kind"
back into humankind.

vivianchinelli.com

"Suffering among nonhuman animals is no less than ours. And it's possible that they suffer even more than many of us do, simply because of their inability to understand what is happening to them, make sense of their plight, escape from it, or alter their conditions."

HOPE FERDOWSIAN, MD

"You don't have to be an 'animal lover.' All you have to agree with is that it's wrong to unnecessarily hurt and kill animals. If you agree with that, you already believe in veganism."

JAMES ASPEY

SLAM, BAM

"Slam, bam and thank you, lamb!"

The faster you shear me,
the worse off I am.

You cut me, you hurt me,
you throw me around.
You're paid for each sheep
as our fleece hits the ground.

There's more to be learned
about how you make wool.
Read about the abuses.
Your head will be full
of "mulesing" information
(a practice so sad).
Just research and find out
what makes it so BAAAAAAD!!

And when I finally cease
producing my fleece,
you'll kill me (you'll "put me to sleep").
So I'll be missing
from your line-up in bed tonight
when you use us, yet again,
to count sheep.

vivianchinelli.com

"You have just dined, and however scrupulously the slaughterhouse is concealed in the graceful distance of miles, there is complicity."

RALPH WALDO EMERSON

"Please don't refuse with your eyes what the animals endure with their bodies."

SHAUN MONSON

DON'T SELL YOURSELF SHORT

"My life without my bacon?!
I can't give up my cheese!!"

Please don't sell yourself short.
You can give up all of these!

If people are willing to risk their lives
for values they hold so deep,
then you can give up bacon and cheese.

Even you can make the leap
from a habit and conditioning
that taught you not to care
for cows and pigs and chickens,
especially when they're not there
right in front of you, behind a wall,
out of sight and out of mind.

The values you cherish
are worth fighting for, too –
to be loving, be just, and be kind.

vivianchinelli.com

"If you want to address climate change, the first thing you do is protect the ocean. And the solution to that is very simple: Leave it alone. If the ocean dies, we all die."

CAPTAIN PAUL WATSON

GOOD GRIEF!

Call it an ocean or a call it the sea.
Between you and me, it doesn't really matter.
Call it the former or call it the latter.
But whatever you call it,
it's in BIG trouble.

"Help!" yelped the kelp!
"Good grief!" cried the dying coral reef!
"Damn!" shouted the clam!

*"Tell me, why are you yelling and
what's all the fuss?"*

Your nets and equipment are killing us!

Our oceans are filled with anger and sadness.
Please stop the destruction and end all this madness!

Look up the "Great Garbage Patch"
and you'll be shocked, I'm sure.
Then you'll ask, "Just how much can our oceans endure?"

The killing, the pollution, the complete disregard
is so bad for our planet.
Don't let down your guard.

Get up, make some noise,
take a stand, and just shout it!
Don't gamble with your future.
Do something about it!

So please act right now and alter our fate.
Go vegan.
Make changes before it's too late.

vivianchinelli.com

"What kind of hobby is mutilation and asphyxiation?"

MEAT YOUR FUTURE

"Now I can look at you in peace; I don't eat you anymore."

FRANZ KAFKA

DID YOU KNOW?

The term "game," mentioned in the following rhyme refers to any wild animal hunted for animal products (primarily meat), for recreation (sporting) or for trophies.

DO UNTO FISH

I flip flop, gasping for breath,
with those around me doing the same.
Why doesn't my plight hurt your heart as much
as when someone goes out to shoot "game?"

When a baby deer's mom is shot and killed,
your eyes want to turn away.
But when a fish gets caught, struggles, then dies,
in *fishing* that's called a "Great Day!"

You cut me with your deboning knife.
I didn't deserve to die.
What gives you the right to end my life?
Have you stopped and just thought to ask why?

You think I'm so insignificant.
You say, "But it's *only* a fish."
I hope you see the connection one day
between me and the death on your dish.

It's seeing connections that will turn your heart
to the person you want to be –
a compassionate soul with respect for all life.
Won't you start by respecting me?

vivianchinelli.com

"Do the best that you can until you know better. Then when you know better, do better."

MAYA ANGELOU

"The world is a dangerous place, not because of those who do evil, but because of those who look on and do nothing."

ALBERT EINSTEIN

DUPED NO MORE

"Don't be silly, animal agriculture is not harming the planet.
Plus, animals don't feel pain, and eating them is healthy.
So don't worry your little head about all that!" say those
who make money off these lies.

They counted on me to not be a thinker.
And that's how they duped me.
Hook, line and sinker.

But I finally made the connection.
Now it's time for a full-on rejection
of the unspeakable things that I do.

There's gonna be some changing
and some serious rearranging.

And I feel better already.
It's true!

So, I'm going vegan for the health of my family.
Going vegan for the health of our planet (our home).
Going vegan for the animals who suffer and die.

Thanks for reading.
That's the end of this poem.

vivianchinelli.com

"You've got to be carefully taught."

LYRICS FROM THE ROGERS AND
HAMMERSTEIN'S SONG "YOU'VE GOT TO BE CAREFULLY TAUGHT"

"None of us ask for fried chicken, pork chops, or ice cream in the delivery room. We were all born without preferences. Everything we think we like, we were taught to like."

DR. MILTON MILLS, MD

DEFINITELY NO!

I asked the young boy,
"Do you eat animals?"

With great surprise to the question, he said, "*NO!*"

"Are you sure?" I asked him one more time.
"And can I explain something before I go?

Did you know that a "nugget" was once a chicken?
Did you know that a burger was a cow?"
Then he asked me what a barbequed rib was.
After I explained, he said, "I get it now."

I could tell he was a thoughtful youngster
who was headed in the right direction.
He told me he would share what
he learned with his friends.
He had finally made the connection!

"I have great hopes for your generation," I told him.
"You will do what mine couldn't achieve.
You'll help abolish these cruel systems
before you grow up.
In that, I just have to believe!"

vivianchinelli.com

"The following rhyme was inspired by my new young friend, Gus. The number 'point 2' (.2) in the rhyme refers to the 1/5th of a pound of meat Gus calculated he'd consume a day if he didn't go vegan. He multiplied that by the number of days from age 12 to age 80. And there you have it! This really cool kid figured out, mathematically, why he had to go vegan!"

VIVIAN CHINELLI

DO THE MATH

At age 12, young Gus,
was much more mature than most of us.

He saw a big problem
and stepped up to the plate (the dinner plate)
and changed what he ate.

He researched how animals were being mistreated.
Up went his hands asking, "What can I do?"

So he started calculating (he loved to do math).
Then he multiplied his days by the number, point 2.

If he lived to be 80, just think of the chickens and cows
that he'd save from the slaughterhouse grounds.

If he didn't go vegan, in 68 years
he'd have eaten as much meat as ***5,000 pounds***!

Problem solved. He'd go vegan.

He would save so much money by not buying meat
and he'd spend it on things that were kind and not cruel.

Compassion into action. He's such a role model
for all of us grown-ups who want to be "cool!"

vivianchinelli.com

"*Every so often I come across statements implying that veganism is a 'white thing.' One night, my husband linked me to an article that tackled that issue head-on. Eating healthy, caring about the environment, and respecting the lives of animals is not a "white thing" at all. It's something that all caring and conscientious people have been doing throughout the history of humankind, all around the world."*

VIVIAN CHINELLI

"*I don't want to be an invisible vegan. I can't teach and uplift others from an invisible place. I want to be the visible black, female, vegan example I wish I had growing up.*"

JASMINE C. LEYVA

IT'S A THING

It's not a *"white thing"*
or a *"black thing."*

It's a *"healthy foods
coming back thing."*

It's a *"try to avoid
a heart attack thing."*

An *"abundance thing."*
Not a *"lack thing."*

It's a *"yummy vegan meal and
snack thing."*

It's a *"keep our climate
on its track thing."*

Finally, *"eating bodies …
is a wack thing!"*

So please won't you join me in the fight,
and do *"the thing"* you know is right?

vivianchinelli.com

"When I travel around the world, I see that poor countries sell their grain to the West while their own children starve in their arms. And we feed it to livestock. So we can eat a steak? Am I the only one who sees this as a crime? Every morsel of meat we eat is slapping the tear-stained face of a starving child. When I look into her eyes, should I be silent? The earth can produce enough for everyone's need. But not enough for everyone's greed."

PHILIP WOLLEN

"We can give people all the information and advice in the world about healthy eating and exercise, but if parents can't buy the food they need to prepare those meals because their only options for groceries are the gas station or the local minimart, then all that is just talk."

MICHELLE OBAMA

FEEDING THE HUNGRY

Is it possible indeed that
we could feed all those in need
if we'd just stop farming animals
and killing them for greed?

The food we could give to hungry kids
goes to farmed animals that we raise.
The majority of the crops we grow,
like wheat and soy and maize,
are sent to farms where cows get fat
while children have little to eat.
They lack the nourishment they deserve
while the rich make their money off "meat."

Though no solution is a perfect one,
we have to start somewhere, and care,
'cause if we don't,
good ol' karma will kick our collective derriere.

If you're not quite ready to think about that,
There's not much more to say
until it starts affecting *you and yours*.
Then let's talk again that day.

vivianchinelli.com

"Pigs in tiny crates suffer beyond anything most of us can easily imagine. They are unable to turn around for weeks at a time, so that their muscles and bones deteriorate. These extremely social and intelligent animals lose their minds from being denied any social or psychological stimulation at all."

RYAN GOSLING

"When I see bacon, I see a pig, I see a little friend, and that's why I can't eat it. Simple as that."

SIR PAUL MCCARTNEY

DO UNTO PIGLETS

Some people think that a piglet's life
is worth nothing more than bacon.
But I think their lives are worth more than that.
And that's the point I'm making.

We cut off their tails so they're not bitten off
by others in their cramped, dark crate.
It's heartbreaking to think that a life of torture
is a piglet's unfortunate fate.

The pain and distress we inflict on them
should cause a big upheaval because
the unthinkable things we do to a pig
are without a doubt, pure evil.

Piglets are ripped from their moms.
Is this something on which we agree?
That if someone did that to us, we'd yell out,
"DON'T YOU DARE EVER DO THAT TO ME!"

The pigs are put in boiling vats
to take off their hair to skin them.
Sometimes they're still conscious
and scream out for help,
with the pain and the fear that is in them!

Like us, they cry when we harass them.
Like us, they wail when we gas them,
which is what we do to take their lives
and then eat while looking right past them.

I hope these emotional words,
make us think when we choose to eat
an innocent pig whose life is worth more
than an unhealthy piece of meat.

vivianchinelli.com

"When I look into the eyes of an animal, I do not see an animal."

ANTHONY DOUGLAS WILLIAMS

"When the suffering of another creature causes you to feel pain ... come closer, as close as you can to him who suffers and try to help him."

LEO TOLSTOY

"An animal's eyes have the power to speak a great language."

MARTIN BUBER

SCARED

I'm a little pig who's terribly scared.
I desperately wish that somebody cared.

This morning we were herded onto a truck.
We're stuck, out of luck, in a system we can't buck.

There's a stench of fear as the truck takes off,
going somewhere, but who knows where.
Trying to squeeze our snouts through the few little slits
where we battle each other for air. I can't breathe.

We squirm and we squeal knowing something's not right.
There's no light. Feels like night.
No end to our struggle in sight. Just fright!
And all I know is I want to take flight. But I can't.

If I squint through the slit
I can see where we're heading and I'm dreading it.
The sign says SLAUGHTERHOUSE.

Already the smell of dying is around me.
No love to surround me. The angel of death has found me.

But wait! The truck has stopped at the gate.
There are some caring people at the entrance
who are giving us water through the slits,
trying to relieve us of the fear. I shed a tear.
My tired eyes thank them for being here, near.

They're opening the gate now and
the truck is jolting forward. It'll be over soon.

Tomorrow another little pig who is terribly scared
will also desperately wish that somebody cared.

vivianchinelli.com

"It is no secret that I am empowered by choosing a plant-based diet. Every time I pass by the meat, eggs and dairy at the market, I say a quiet 'No, thank you.' I feel a rush of satisfaction that my dollars that day will support a healthier world--and that every single meal is an opportunity to do less harm and more good (and, boy, do I love opportunities!)."

SUZY AMIS CAMERON

"Veganism is not a 'sacrifice.' It is a joy."

GARY L. FRANCIONE

PROCRASTINATED

Animals are crated,
mutilated, violated, annihilated,
dinner plated.
Milk is made into cheese and grated.

Indoctrinated! Salivated.
"Meat" was served and so I ate it.

(Now that I'm vegan...)
Why'd I wait? Procrastinated.
Being vegan is **under**-rated.

And I thought that I would hate it.
But instead, I celebrate it!!
It's my life now, wouldn't trade it
for a single thing I ate.

It was fated, 'though belated.
Took me years, but finally made it.
Vegan now and so elated.
I gotta say it – it feels great!

vivianchinelli.com

"But for the sake of some little mouthful of flesh we deprive a soul of the sun and light, and of that proportion of life and time it had been born into the world to enjoy."

PLUTARCH

"The time will come when men such as I will look upon the murder of animals as they now look upon the murder of men."

LEONARDO DA VINCI

"Insanity is doing the same things over and over and expecting different results."

ALBERT EINSTEIN

THE NEW TALK

"Hey Mom, Dad, I think it's time we have The Talk."

These days … our kids won't be asking
for the "Birds and the Bees" talk
or the "Can I borrow the keys?" talk,
if you know what I mean.

They'll ask about the climate
and our treatment of animals,
the lies they've been told
and the indifference they've seen.

What about all the foods that we fed them
(the ones that might have caused cancer)?
Will we find some way to justify that?
Tell me, how are we planning to answer?

They'll ask us about
all the choices we've made.
They'll want to know
why we left them betrayed
by doing the same old things
day-after-day
and expecting a different outcome.
INSANITY!

So be prepared for *The Talk*.
Start your research right now.
Don't sit around doing zero.
Align your values with your actions
so when it's time for *The Talk*,
you'll undoubtedly be your kid's hero.

vivianchinelli.com

"That which you hate to be done to you, do not do to another."

THE GOLDEN RULE (CAN BE FOUND IN SOME
FORM IN ALMOST EVERY ETHICAL TRADITION)

"Children learn more from what you are than what you teach."

W.E.B. DU BOIS

YOUNG DAD GOES VEGAN

When Ricardo became a dad,
things changed and priorities got rearranged.

He started reading and watching
and listening and growing.
Started questioning his ethics
and gained a deep sense of knowing
that adopting new values
was an important endeavor
that would better the life
of his precious girl, Perla,
forever.

vivianchinelli.com

"We're doing our best to set them up for success in their bodies as they are growing. I also tell my children that it is worthwhile to make sacrifices for a greater good. Our capacity as humans is that we operate at a very high cognitive level where we can make decisions about things that we love which we are choosing to refrain from."

MAYIM BIALEK

"We choose to eat meat and have therefore built slaughterhouses for the animals and hospitals for us."

AKBARALI JETHA

FEEDING OUR CHILDREN

Heart disease and cancer.
Do you think that there's a chance you're
setting up your kids for getting those
when you feed them meat?

Allergies from dairy. Diabetes is so scary.
Have you thought about the impact
of the toxic foods they eat?

Our job is to protect our kids
and keep them safe from harm, but
you'll increase their risk of illness
serving animals that are farmed.

So, try to prevent those things by nurturing
their bodies as they grow.
Serve plant-based foods
on which they'll thrive.
What a great gift you'll bestow!

In addition to the gift of health,
you'll be teaching them empathy.
Then they'll open their hearts
to the weakest among us.

Sit back and just watch, wait and see,
that your child will be conscious
of things much greater
than cell phones and media distraction.

They'll be focused on
making this world so much better,
putting our most-cherished values …
into action.

vivianchinelli.com

"The surest path toward discovering your purpose is to say 'NO' along the way to what doesn't feel aligned with your heart."

EVE ROSENBERG

COGNITIVE DISSONANCE

When we say we love animals
but eat them.
When we say we hate cruelty
but pay to mistreat them.
That's cognitive dissonance.

She considered herself non-violent.
Said she wouldn't hurt a fly.
Yet when it came to her craving for bacon,
she was like, "**DIE PIG, DIE!**"

A little spider in his bathroom?
He gently escorted her out.
But he'd kill a cow for a burger.
Tell me, what do you think
that's all about?

Cognitive dissonance, my dear friend.
If we don't address it now,
it'll bite us in the end.

When we align our values with our actions,
there's no more need for excuses.
Let's start "walking our talk"
and stop supporting abuses.

I know we can do it!

vivianchinelli.com

"And God said: Behold, I have given you every herb yielding seed which is upon the face of all the earth, and every tree that has seed-yielding fruit. To you it shall be for food."

ONE OF THE TRANSLATIONS OF GENESIS 1:29

"We are here to heal, not harm. We are here to love, not hate. We are here to create, not destroy."

ANTHONY DOUGLAS WILLIAMS

STREET CONVERSATION

One day an activist went out for her walk.
She met three young ladies. They started to talk.

"Scripture commands we eat animals," one said
(and she said it so very sincerely).

Then the activist answered, "I don't know Scripture,
but it sounds like you know it, quite clearly.

So, especially you, you'll love to read
the article I wish to suggest.
It's called 'Life After Brisket,' in Tablet Magazine.
It puts an important commandment to the test.

Find that article on the internet.
Then I hope you'll understand
that **not** torturing animals
is what God would command."

They thanked her for her insights.
She thanked them for their time
(not knowing they'd end up in her very next rhyme).

vivianchinelli.com

"God loved the birds and invented trees. Man loved the birds and invented cages."

JACQUES DEVAL

"Man is the most insane species. He worships an invisible God and destroys a visible Nature, unaware that the Nature he is destroying is this God that he is worshipping."

UNKNOWN

GOD'S FIRST CHOICE

To the religious, the Christian,
the Muslim and the Jew.

Are you sure God approves
of these cruel things we do?

Please revisit your sources,
and I hope that you'll find
that God's first choice
is that we be loving and kind.

vivianchinelli.com

"One of the most important life lessons that I taught my kindergarten students was, 'Don't take things that aren't yours.'"

VIVIAN CHINELLI

WHAT ABOUT HONEY?

*"Why exactly do vegans
choose not to eat honey?
After all, don't bees make it for us?
They make it, we take it
and bake honey cake.
It's no biggie.
Come on, what's the fuss?"*

Well, the truth is that bees *don't* make honey for us.
But we seem to take what wasn't earned.
We were taught not to do that in kindergarten class.
I guess it was a lesson not learned.

Biggie or not, the mindset's the same.
Don't take what's not yours.
Please don't play that game.
It starts with an insect as small as a bee.
Then grows into a cherished value
we call *empathy*.

vivianchinelli.com

"When people ask me why I don't eat meat or any other animal products, I say, 'Because they are unhealthy and they are the product of a violent and inhumane industry.'"

CASEY AFFLECK

FOIE GRAS (fwäh gräh)

They say it's a delicacy in French cuisine.
But it's the "fat liver" of a brutalized and forced fed duck!

What the ****?!

"When I turned vegan, I didn't feel that way about every animal around. I've noticed it's something that changes naturally. Nowadays I vacuum around a spider, catch flies to release them outside, and let silverfish go about their business; a whole new world, a whole new-found mental peace. I love being vegan; it's the best thing that ever happened to me. I finally understand, we all have but one life, human, cow, ant, everyone. It is not our right to take it away on a whim, simply because we can; it's their right to live their lives, just like us, just like me."

JACO VAN DRONGELEN

"I found this beautiful quote, above, credited to someone named Jaco, but couldn't find any other reference to him. If anyone knows Jaco, please give him a big hug from me. I, too, vacuum around spiders and let insects go. I've been doing that my whole life."

VIVIAN CHINELLI

IN A VEGAN WORLD

In a vegan world, I won't be called "*that* vegan,"
'cause we'll all have the same point of view.

Compassionate giving. Respect for the living.
I dream of that world. How 'bout you?

"*Everyone says, 'I don't eat a lot of meat, dairy and eggs.' The truth is you don't know how much you eat until you stop.*"

COLLEEN PATRICK-GOUDREAU

IN MODERATION

I've often heard people say,
"I don't eat a lot of animal products.
Hey, life's all about moderation."

"Everything in moderation"
is the motto of every generation.
But it doesn't hold water
if it's used as excuses
for supporting a system
that's fraught with abuses.

Paying for cruelty on Wednesday through Sunday,
but not eating animals on Tuesday or Monday
may sound good to us but not to the calves
who on Wednesday through Sunday
are sliced into halves.

There's no gray area here.
It's either black or white,
day or night,
wrong or right,
cold or hot.
Support these systems, or not.

So in the end
there can't be a *yes* and *no* combination,
for any abuse in moderation.

Now if eating in moderation
is the first step on your journey
with a goal to stop cruelty in the end.
Then I encourage you to hurry.
There are animals that need you.
There's a calf out there for you to defend!

vivianchinelli.com

"Intellectually, human beings and animals may be different, but it's pretty obvious that animals have a rich emotional life and that they feel joy and pain. It's easy to forget the connection between a hamburger and the cow it came from. But I forced myself to acknowledge the fact that every time I ate a hamburger, a cow had ceased to breathe."

MOBY

"I watched a TV documentary about how animals were farmed, killed, and prepared for us to eat. I saw all those cows and pigs and realized I couldn't be a part of it anymore. It was horrible. I did some research to make sure I could still obtain enough protein to fight and, once satisfied that I could, I stopped. I'll never go back."

DAVID HAYE

OUR CHOICE

Our choice to buy a steak
means a cow has to die.

If we choose to serve bacon,
a pig suffers. No lie.

Our choice to eat chicken?
If you knew the truth, you would cry.

And by the time we cut a fish
with our deboning knife,
he's lost his last struggle to save his own life.

But now, here's the good news.

You can make other choices
and still feel joyful and alive.
Leave out animals and eat plant-based.
Then be amazed how you'll thrive!

It's a **heart** choice,
not a hard choice to go vegan, my friend.
And just think of the compassionate message you'll send.

vivianchinelli.com

"Choose a compassionate frame of mind. Always choose love. Always be kind."

BETH ARNOLD

"It takes nothing away from a human to be kind to an animal."

JOAQUIN PHOENIX

"Teach compassion. Model empathy. Inspire action."

VIVIAN CHINELLI

LITTLE MISS MUFFET

(Another Mother Goose Nursery Rhyme Goes Vegan)

Little Miss Muffet sat on her tuffet,
eating her curds and whey.

Then along came a spider who reminded her
that she could have eaten
a much more compassionate meal.

So, she went vegan the very next day.

vivianchinelli.com

"Some people think the 'plant-based whole foods diet' is extreme. Half a million people a year will have their chests opened up and a vein taken from their leg and sewn on their coronary artery. Some would call that extreme."

DR. CALDWELL ESSELSTYN, MD

"Animals are not ingredients."

BARBARA THOMPSON

"The thing I always tell people, if you need a recipe every time you cook, that means you don't trust yourself. So spend time trusting yourself a little bit in the kitchen. You put a little bit of that, little bit of that. That's why when I cook, I always say, 'like so, like that,' because it ain't got to be exact. Have fun with it. Think about, 'What do I want to taste? What do I got a taste for?' And trust that your palate is going to lead you."

TABITHA BROWN

A VEGAN TWIST

Vegan chicken salad.
What a perfect dish.
Finger lickin' (without the dead chicken).
So healthy and delish!

Mac and cheese? My favorite, please!
A comfort food at last.
With a vegan twist, it's on my list.
I'm so very glad you asked.

Don't get nervous and sweaty
that your favorite food, spaghetti, is off limits,
'cause that isn't true.
With no eggs on the label
it's fit for your table
with veggies and lots of ragú
(the vegan version, of course).

I adore chocolate!!!!
Need I say more?
Chocolate cake. I love to bake.
Chocolate cookies are fun to make.
No dairy or eggs, and it won't be "fake."
JUST CHOCOLATE! CHOCOLATE! CHOCOLATE!

There are so many vegan versions
of the foods that you so crave.
With a few little tweaks, in no time at all,
they'll soon become your *fave*.

So please do check the internet.
Be wowed by abundance of choice.
Eat nutritiously. Eat voraciously.
Eat deliciously. **REJOICE!**

vivianchinelli.com

"Veganism has given me a higher level of awareness and spirituality, primarily because the energy associated with eating has shifted to other areas. If you are violent to yourself by putting things into your body that violate its spirit, it will be difficult not to perpetuate that [violence] onto someone else."

DEXTER SCOTT KING

"Turkeys are some of the most gentle creatures in the world, and 46 million of them are killed every Thanksgiving."

BILLIE EILISH

I'M NOT VEGAN BUT MY COUSIN IS

TURKEY TALK

It's almost Thanksgiving.
My chances of living past Thursday
have gone up in smoke.

I don't want to die.
So I must ask you why is it
you treat my life as a joke?

You cut me, then gut me,
stick bread up my butt. Gee,
is this how you celebrate life?

What a sad way to go.
I just hope that you know
I don't want to be sliced by your knife.

You can make new traditions.
I know you are able.
I'd be so very happy
to stay off your table.

Be grateful with a plateful
of respect and compassion.
Make Thanksgiving … Thanks*Living*,
and start a new fashion.

Please!

vivianchinelli.com

"The following rhyme was inspired by a phone conversation with a new vegan friend. She had been invited to share Thanksgiving with a good friend of hers who, as predicted, would be serving a turkey for dinner.

My friend was not only feeling extremely sad that a turkey's life would be taken for the meal, but that her friend, who also said she loved animals, wasn't feeling any remorse about it."

VIVIAN CHINELLI

ALONE

She called me last night in her sadness,
feeling alone, facing all of this madness.
"You're not alone," I consoled her,
"though it might feel like it.
There are others out there
who, like you, won't permit
this cruelty to persist.
And like you, are taking action,
speaking up for the animals
'til they get satisfaction."

To those out there who aren't vegan,
I know that you care, but are scared
to make changes so late.
But I did it. It's great to do great things
that you never dared.

vivianchinelli.com

"I am grateful to realize that my desires do not entitle me to add to another's suffering."

ZOE WEIL

"Sometimes we might remember that all other animals have every bit as much right to be here and to be unmolested as any human does."

DAVID ATTENBOROUGH

"They beg for mercy. Are you listening?"

JOEY CARBSTRONG

DO UNTO CHICKENS

I'm a 6-week-old chicken you'll soon pay to kill.
Then you'll call me a "broiler" (or "fryer").
With no thoughtful regard for my suffering,
I'll be thrown on your BBQ fire.

You cram me in this space with the others
and cut our beaks off so we cannot peck.
We wallow around in our urine and poop.
And you're eating us?! What the heck!!

I've heard of those places called "free-range" farms,
with small doors that lead out to the yard.
But "free-range" doesn't mean anything,
if getting out is impossibly hard!

It's all marketing. Check into it.
Ask why male chicks are **shredded-alive** to be killed.
It's an accepted standard practice in this sinister system
to ensure that your desire for our flesh is fulfilled.

In nature, we birds will lay an egg,
once a year, maybe now and then.
But with genetic modification,
you have "Frankensteined" the hen!

Calcium is leached from our bones
whenever a mama hen lays an egg for your breakfast.
We work so damn hard
for three hundred and sixty-five days.

We can barely stand up; our bones are so brittle.
If you don't do the research, you'll stay knowing little
about all the horrors we chickens go through.
Who will it be up to, to care, if not you?

vivianchinelli.com

"I don't see why someone should lose their life so you can have a snack."

RUSSELL BRAND

"If I'm eating food I know was a creature in a cage, it brings up memories of segregation and the stories from my ancestors, of being in captivity and denied their personalities, their true beings. Animals were not made for us, or our use. They have their own use, which is just being who they are."

ALICE WALKER

WHAT'S THE DEAL?

"What's the deal?
It can't be real!

Trading an innocent animal's
WHOLE LIFE OF SUFFERING
for my 5-minute meal?!

Wow! What a steal!"

****

Where is our compassion?
Why don't we end this madness?
How can we let this happen?
Why don't we feel the sadness?

What has died inside of us
that lets this stuff go on?
Our connection to the earth
and its inhabitants is gone.

vivianchinelli.com

> "Until he extends the circle of his compassion to all living things, man will not find himself in peace."

ALBERT SCHWEITZER

> "I am determined not to kill, not to let others kill, and not to support any act of killing in the world. We should consume in such a way that helps to reduce the suffering of living beings. And that way we can preserve compassion in our hearts."

THICH NHAT HANH

CIRCLE OF COMPASSION

They drew their circle of compassion.

Puppies are in, piglets are out.
Kittens are in, calves are out.
Most birds are in, but not chickens, they're out.
Is that what compassion is all about?

We teach our children *Be kind to animals.*
Do unto others as you want done.

So are you still willing to take a life?
Or are you going to be the one
who "walks the talk,"
who's ready to grow your circle of compassion
to include all animals and be a hero
who fights for each, precious life,
with passion?

vivianchinelli.com

"As mothers to companion animals or human beings, we are better than eating the flesh of animals who never felt the sun on their backs or were (never) given the chance to live in an environment where they weren't filthy, scared, deprived of clean air or room to even sit comfortably, or turn around. I'm sorry, you can't be a feminist and drink dairy or eat meat. So, my advice is to better yourselves."

SIMONE REYES

"Nothing's changed my life more. I feel better about myself as a person being conscious and responsible for my actions and I lost weight and my skin cleared up and I got bright eyes and I just became stronger and healthier and happier. Can't think of anything better in the world to be but be vegan."

ALICIA SILVERSTONE

LISTEN UP

Listen to your vegan wife.
Eat plant-based and save a life.

Listen to your vegan man.
Believe him when he says you can.

Listen to your vegan friends.
And put an end to violence.

Listen to your vegan kid.
You can do it if they did.

Listen to your vegan boss.
Giving up meat is a healthy loss.

Listen to your vegan dad.
Go vegan now and make him glad.

Listen to your vegan mom.
ALWAYS listen to your vegan mom!

vivianchinelli.com

"Animal farming is not humane, in any way, shape or form."

INGRID NEWKIRK

"Non-violence leads to the highest ethics, which is the goal of all evolution. Until we stop harming other living beings, we are still savages."

THOMAS EDISON

BEST FRIENDS

Dog and Calf were two best friends
who roamed the farm, together.
Dog became the family pet
while Calf became burgers and leather.

"But we're just a small farm!"
cried Dog to the farmer.
"We even gave Calf a name."

"Sorry," said the farmer,
"when it comes to making a profit,
the fate of all calves is the same."

So, if your heart's set on burgers or leather,
remember Calf's life at the end.
Then ask if your habits
are more important than the loss
of a dog's dear and very best friend.

vivianchinelli.com

"Animal factories are one more sign of the extent to which our technological capacities have advanced faster than our ethics."

PETER SINGER

"You have to hold out hope that someone will listen, that people can change."

EMILY MORAN BARWICK

DID YOU KNOW?

Factory farms, mentioned in the following rhyme, are large industrialized complexes on which up to thousands of animals are raised indoors in crammed conditions intended to maximize production at minimal cost. While animals are allowed more space on smaller farms, they ultimately meet the same fate as those raised in factory farms.

INTERVIEW WITH FACTORY FARMED ANIMALS

Reporter to Pig:
Would you like to say something to the public?

Pig:
HELP! I'M SUFFERING! WE'RE SUFFERING!

Reporter to Cow:
Oh, that's awful!

Cow:
PLEASE!! DO SOMETHING!

Reporter to Chicken:
Oh my goodness. Tell me what I can do to help.

Chicken:
I think that you already know.
***ABOLISH THIS VIOLENT HORROR SHOW!
ANIMAL FARMING HAS GOT TO GO!***

Reporter to All:
*I've heard your plea, and I strongly agree!
I'll do what I can to make the whole world see
that disrespecting your lives is cruel and unjust.
I've got to spread the message to all.* ***I MUST!***

"*The greatness of a nation and its moral progress can be judged by the way its animals are treated.*"

MAHATMA GANDHI

DID YOU KNOW?

In the egg industry, male chicks have no monetary value. They won't produce eggs and don't have the right body structure for "meat" production." So, within hours of their hatching, male chicks are disposed of by electrocution, gassing, or by being grinded up (shredded) alive.

IN SHORT

LIFE OF A FARMED ANIMAL, IN SHORT

Bred.
Fed.
Then off with his/her head.
Dead.
Bled.
Sanitized.
Then fed (to us).

LIFE OF A MALE CHICK, IN SHORT

DAY ONE

Bred.
Shred.
Dead.
Sadly, no tears shed.

Enough said.

vivianchinelli.com

"You can't do anything violent humanely."

JAMES WILDMAN, M. ED

DID YOU KNOW?

Ag-Gag laws, mentioned in the following rhyme, are anti-whistle blower laws that apply within the agriculture industries. The term typically refers to U.S. state laws that forbid undercover filming or photography of activities on animal farms without consent of their owners. This law particularly targets whistle blowers of animal rights abuses, at these facilities.

AG-GAG

"STOP! *You're not allowed to film in here!*
Don't you know it's against the law?
You can't video animal abuses like this
and then show the world what you saw."

Why?
What are you hiding in there?

"Better you don't know.
Better you don't care.

Anyway, it's the law.
AG-GAG."

"There's one thing that Rudy, Truffles, and Terrin have in common with nearly all the other pigs (at Farm Sanctuary): they can't stand the sound of clanking metal. Even though they were very young, they must remember what it was like to be crowded behind metal slats on that transport truck. They hate the very sound of trucks. When the UPS truck drives up to the farm, they run and hide. It's a reminder of how sensitive and intelligent pigs are and that, while they may forgive, they don't forget."

GENE BAUR

While inspecting a slaughterhouse for water waste, "I suddenly came across these piles of hooves and heads and hearts and bones. I was startled and didn't know quite what to do. ... it was a terrible moment. I was trying to maintain my sanity by saying 'but they are only animals,' but it didn't work."

ALEX HERSHAFT

PLACES

SLAUGHTERHOUSES
Violent places.
Callous faces.
Kindness? No traces.
Just disgraces!

FARM SANCTUARIES FOR RESCUED ANIMALS
Peaceful places.
Friendly faces.
Safe spaces.
Warm embraces.

vivianchinelli.com

"I can't think if anything that makes me happier than seeing an animal's contentment, witnessing a creature allowed to be who he wants to be in the world – and at peace. It's a thing of beauty."

JENNY BROWN

"Take a little break and bring joy to your heart by watching heartwarming videos of protected and happy animals with their families and friends.

Go to Kinderworld.org. From the Menu, choose Videos, then Happy Animals."

VIVIAN CHINELLI

I'M NOT VEGAN BUT MY COUSIN IS

HAPPY ANIMALS

Take a break from the heartache
and watch happy animals play.

I could do that all day!

viviachinelli.com

"All of the things we desire in our lives: love, care, safety, freedom, joy, affection and happiness are denied from animals, all so we can take from them what wasn't even ours to begin with."

JOEY CARBSTRONG

HEY DIDDLE DIDDLE

(Another Mother Goose Nursery Rhyme Goes Vegan)

Hey diddle diddle.
The calf and the fiddle.
The cow jumped over the moon.

She was escaping with her daughter
to avoid that day's slaughter
which would make them into ground beef by noon.

Hey diddle diddle.
The calf and the fiddle.
The cow jumped over the moon.

Just look to your heart.
You'll know where to start.
And you're bound to be vegan real soon.

vivianchinelli.com

"The following rhyme contains the transcript of a discussion between a thoughtful five-year old girl and an adult (maybe her mom). Your heart will just melt as this little girl stands up for something she strongly believes in – protecting animals. I might be wrong, but I think we all start life with the kind of empathy this little girl exhibits. What happens to us next, as we age, usually depends on how we are conditioned by society, friends and family.

Search the internet for "I Won't Eat Animals, Girl Tells Her Mother."

VIVIAN CHINELLI

"Learning to stand in somebody else's shoes to see through their eyes, that's how peace begins."

PRESIDENT BARACK OBAMA

A FIVE-YEAR-OLD SPEAKS

She'll make you say "Ahhhh,"
and for sure drop your jaw
at her very steadfast conviction.

She caught on before 6,
that she didn't need a fix
of society's cruel, meat addiction.

Girl:
I like animals. I won't eat chicken and meat!

Mom:
What about fish?

Girl:
Fish, uhm. Is fish an animal?

Mom:
Yeah.

Girl:
I won't eat that either!

Mom:
Oh my gosh.

Girl:
I won't eat animals!
I think that they don't like being cooked in ovens!

vivianchinelli.com

"Animals are my friends. And I don't eat my friends."

GEORGE BERNARD SHAW

MARY HAD A LITTLE LAMB

(Another Mother Goose Nursery Rhyme Goes Vegan)

Mary loved a little lamb.
His fleece was white as snow.
But here's a thing,
a secret thing that Mary didn't know.

When Mary went to school one day,
they snuck her lamb to slaughter.
Yet Mary wasn't told the truth.
"He's lost," they told their daughter.

When Mary grew up,
she learned how Lamb
had met his tragic fate.
Her parents confessed
that her friend had become the dinner
that night on her plate.

This really shook-up Mary.
She finally understood.
And swore to be a vegan.
Good!

vivianchinelli.com

"*I made the choice to be vegan because I will not eat (or wear, or use) anything that could have an emotional response to its death or captivity. I can well imagine what that must feel like for our non-human friends – the fear, the terror, the pain – and I will not cause such suffering to a fellow living being.*"

RAI AREN

BUT I'M VEGETARIAN ALREADY

But I'm vegetarian, so for sure I thought you'd be thrilled
that I don't eat animals who were abused and then killed.

Every day I rejoice that because of my choice,
no throat has been cut and no blood has been spilled.

But wait, what?

Are you telling me that farmers are selling me
the myth that there's no killing in eggs and in dairy?

That we kill mama cows and all egg-laying chickens
(and their **babies**)?! Heck, that's so darn wicked and scary!

So, I gather you'd rather I research the matter.
Which I will, 'cause I must do the right thing at last.

No halfway commitment to kindness and justice.
My paying for violence will be a thing of the past.

(And later that night …)

I did what you suggested. There was so much I learned
about dairy and eggs, that got me concerned.

When it comes to those industries, it's both slavery *and* slaughter!
(I'd scream if you did that to *my* mom or daughter!)

I do see your point and I'm thinking I oughta
be vegan and stay consistent with my values.

Yeh, I GOTTA!

vivianchinelli.com

"Only when we have become non-violent towards all life will we have learned to live well ourselves."

CESAR CHAVEZ

"All oppression is connected."

STACEYANN CHIN

"Every moment is an organizing opportunity, every person a potential activist, every minute a chance to change the world."

DOLORES HUERTA

BOYCOTT

I'm boycotting systems
of cruelty and violence.
It makes sense
to get off the fence,
to stand up and speak out.
Without a doubt,
it's the right thing to do.

"A man of my spiritual intensity does not eat corpses."

GEORGE BERNARD SHAW

"My body will not be a tomb for other creatures."

LEONARDO DI VINCI

TO EAT OR NOT TO EAT

TO EAT: Cherries and berries, quinoa and rices. Bok choy and tofu with lots of good spices. Walnuts and almonds, red peppers and beets. Cauliflower, beans, and some dark chocolate treats. Bananas, potatoes, red onions, tomatoes. Cabbage and jams, edamame and yams. Squashes and peanuts, smoothies and tea. Pea soup and eggplant, a peach off a tree. Oranges, corn, avocado and melon. I try to eat all of the good foods they're sellin'. Ice cream from coconut, yogurt from soy. A plethora of choices. Let's eat and enjoy!

NOT TO EAT: Any corpse of the following, I will not be swallowing: a tiger, a chicken, a chipmunk or cow. A rabbit, a turkey, a snake or a sow. A dog or a fish or an elephant's trunk. A lion, a lamb or a real smelly skunk! A horse or a pangolin, peacock or pheasant. A leopard or monkey. That doesn't sound pleasant! A rat or a bat, or a lobster or two. A buffalo, cat, or a young kangaroo. A parakeet, duck, a whale or a deer. My body's not a graveyard, of that I am clear.

P.S. I'll also skip eggs 'cause they're not necessary. And I won't be having dairy 'cause dairy is scary.

vivianchinelli.com

"Our task must be to widen our circle of compassion to embrace all living creatures and the whole of nature and its beauty."

ALBERT EINSTEIN

"When you feel the suffering of every living thing in your own heart, that is consciousness."

SHRIMAD BHAGAVAD GITA (HINDU SCRIPTURE)

A FISH SPEAKS

When you come to the ocean,
wade, swim or sunbathe.
Just please don't invade
with your Fishing Trade.

When you do,
you're not only killing me,
but you're killing the others
that live in the sea.
It's a tragedy!

The dolphins, the whales
and the porpoises, too,
are injured or killed
by the things that you do.
Killing trillions (yes, ***trillions!***)
of fish every year
will impact the future for your kids, I fear.

Watch documentaries.
Listen closely and learn all about it.
You'll wonder how in earth's name
you ever allowed it.

So, play in the sand,
float or snorkel and surf
but don't come down under
and demolish my turf.

I have faith that you'll save us.
On that I'll depend,
especially if you're vegan,
my forward-looking friend.

vivianchinelli.com

"When a man wantonly destroys one of the works of man we call him a vandal. When he destroys one of the works of God we call him a 'Sportsman.'"

JOSEPH WOOD KRUTCH

CATCH AND RELEASE (A FISH TALE)

I know it seems noble to catch and release.
No killing was done in your view.
But we're more prone to die
once you toss us back in
'cause all of the things that you do.

Think how we feel when we're reeled on your boat.
Sharp hooks pierce our gut and our throat.

Our pain might be different
than yours, as a human,
but indeed, we feel pain.
Please take note.

You handle and de-hook us.
We can't breathe. We're distressed.
Your actions make us vulnerable
so we can't do our best when
fleeing from a predator that we must avoid.
Our best chance for survival?
Sadly, destroyed!

If you want to exhibit compassion,
let us be, let us swim, let us roam.
Go out on your boat but read or talk while you float.
Just keep your hooks out of our watery home.

You say, "fishing is tension releasing."
That it's peaceful and such a great sport.
But it's violent to me
and I'd rather you release all your tension
on a basketball court!

vivianchinelli.com

"Nothing more will benefit our Earth and human health as much as the vegan diet."

LED

"Vegan food is soul food in its truest form. Soul food means to feed the soul. And, to me, your soul is your truest intent. If your intent is pure, you are pure."

ERYKAH BADU

VEGAN RESTAURANTS

Vegan Restaurants.
Flourishing and Nourishing.
Encouraging!

"Let food be thy medicine and medicine be thy food,"
said Hippocrates, physician of old.

So if you want healthy food and *food for the soul*,
then visit a place where that food will be sold.
If you haven't gone yet, come on, be bold
and visit a vegan restaurant.

You'll be so happy you did!

But if you can't find a vegan restaurant,
there are others that have vegan dishes.
Ask the server to point out some options for you
that are plant-based, nutritious and delicious!

vivianchinelli.com

"I know what the caged bird feels, alas."

PAUL LAURENCE DUNBAR (SON OF SLAVES)

"Caged birds accept each other, but flight is what they long for."

TENNESSEE WILLIAMS

PARAKEET PETER

Memories of you, Peter,
are, alas, bittersweet.
When I was young, long before
there was Twitter and tweet.

They clipped your wings before they sold you,
so that you couldn't fly.
And I kept you in a cage so that you wouldn't try.

I'm terribly sorry, precious Peter,
for the way I made you live.
You were special and deserved better.

Signing off.
With love,
Viv

P.S.
And sorry, little goldfish, that your short life was spent in a tiny glass bowl, swimming in circles and going nowhere. Finally, Schultz, my furry little hamster friend, I can imagine now what it felt like to be restrained by the restrictions I put on your movement, back when you lived in a small cage. I apologize for that, too!

vivianchinelli.com

"Never believe that animals suffer less than humans. Pain is the same for us. Even worse, because they cannot help themselves."

LOUIS J. CAMUTI

"After I became vegan, I started wondering if, and yes, assuming, that veterinarians were not only vegans, but proud and outspoken ones. How could they not be? All the vets I knew were caring and kind to my beloved fur babies, always looking after their best interest, always ready to try anything to relieve their suffering.

When I discovered the reality that a very small percentage of vets were vegan, honestly, I was surprised and saddened. I wrote the following rhyme in response to that discovery."

VIVIAN CHINELLI

ANIMAL DOCS

Dear Vets of Our Pets,

We adore you!
You took an oath to keep animals from harm.
But still most of you defend that it doesn't extend
to the suffering on an animal farm.

You use a scalpel to relieve our fur babies from pain.
But use a knife to cut up "meat" and you call it humane.

While I adore you, I implore you
to rethink your choices.
Extend your kindness to unloved animals
and be a force for their voices.

Thank you.

vivianchinelli.com

"Ask the experimenters why they experiment on animals, and the answer is, 'Because the animals are like us.' Ask the experimenters why it is morally okay to experiment on animals, and the answer is, 'Because the animals are not like us.'"

CHARLES MAGEL

TESTING 1, 2, 3

I'm a docile and trusting animal
who's done nothing to you, and yet
you performed an agonizing experiment on me today.

You pulled me out of my cramped cage
and sprayed something harsh directly into my eyes.

I cried.

Tomorrow you'll do the same.
Who's to blame for this cruel game?

You experiment on millions of animals,
including monkeys and puppies and birds.
The anguish you put us through every day
cannot be explained in words.

There are alternate ways to do research now.
Please support them and do what is right.
Like you, I want to live my life in peace.
Won't you stand up and help me fight?!

vivianchinelli.com

"Beagles are routinely blinded in the testing of shampoo and soap. Think about that in the shower."

BLUE CROSS OF INDIA FACEBOOK PAGE

THE LEAPING BUNNY SPEAKS

My important job is to guarantee
that the product you're buying
is cruelty-free (no animal testing).

So look for me.
I'm that iconic Leaping Bunny.

I'll be on your cleanser,
your make-up, and more.
Your compassionate choice
is what I'm aiming for.

Now go and explore
all the choices in store
that display me –
the cruelty-free bunny.

And please don't forget to check the ingredients for animal "by-products." While I guarantee no animal testing, I can't guarantee a vegan product. I'm doing what I can. Thanks very much for helping!

vivianchinelli.com

"Being vegan is a glorious adventure. It touches every aspect of my life – my relationships, how I relate to the world."

VICTORIA MORAN

GET ON BOARD

Get on board the vegan train!

It's moving fast
and you will find
if you don't jump on,
you'll be left behind.

The movement is growing,
folks are getting on board.
With a new sense of purpose
we're working toward
a world in which we fight for all others.
We can do it together,
my sisters and brothers.

Let's stand up for our health.
Stand up for our planet.
Stand up for the animals,
and each other! Gosh dammit.

vivianchinelli.com

"Behind every beautiful fur coat, there is a story. It's a bloody story."

MARY TYLER MOORE

"Nobody really needs a mink coat ... except the mink!"

GLENDA JACKSON

BORN TO BE ME

I was born to be me,
not your shoe or your glove,
not a purse to hold money,
not a stole made of mink.

Not the coat that you wear,
or your chair made of leather.
So please STOP when you shop
and take a moment to think.

Let me stay in my skin
and please, you stay in yours.
Think man-made and buy "faux" (foh)
It's the rage!
You'll be changing the way
that we think of our choices.
You'll be ushering in a new age.

Won't that be wonderful?!

And, oh yes,
sometimes the fake stuff looks so very real,
so let people know that it's faux.
Or buy things that don't look like animal skins
and you'll look like a cruelty-free pro.

vivianchinelli.com

"We do not need to eat animals, wear animals, or use animals for entertainment purposes, and our only defense of these uses is our pleasure, amusement and convenience."

GARY FRANCIONE

"Using animals for entertainment is big business, plain and simple. And it must be stopped."

JANE VELEZ-MITCHELL

BAD BEHAVIOR

Cockfight, bullfight,
greyhound racing isn't right.

Performing dolphins in a pool.
Elephants doing handstands, cruel!

Wild animals who are raised and caged
in habitats that are fake and staged.

Rodeo stunts like calf roping,
horseracing and animal doping.

Making bulls run through a town.
Frightened foxes hunted down.

When will our lack of empathy end?
When will people stop defending
exploitation and bad behavior?

Please speak up and be their savior.

vivianchinelli.com

"Animals give me more pleasure through the viewfinder of a camera than they ever did in the crosshairs of a gunsight. And after I've finished 'shooting,' my unharmed victims are still around for others to enjoy. I have developed a deep respect for animals. I consider them fellow living creatures with certain rights that should not be violated any more than those of humans."

JIMMY STEWART

READY, AIM, TAKE A LIFE

If I know one thing about hunting,
it's that for some folks it's a fun thing.
Maybe that's why the victims are called "game."

But whether it's fun or not,
an innocent victim gets shot.
Whether it's an elephant or a deer
or a fox filled with fear,
the result for the victim's the same.

Exhilaration. Overpopulation. Wildlife conservation.
Hunters use these three excuses as a reason
to buy shotguns and then take an innocent life
when the government declares hunting season.

My debate skills on hunting are limited,
but there are some videos you should see.
I implore you.
Just search "Earthling Ed's Thoughts About Hunting."
And I promise that he will not bore you.

Learn about different viewpoints.
Both sides will be stated.
(Intelligent debate can be so underrated.)
I hope you get a chance to watch him today.
Then let's get those rifles stored safely away.

P.S.
And I know you don't need coaching
about the horrors of wildlife poaching.

vivianchinelli.com

"*The problem is that humans have victimized animals to such a degree that they are not even considered victims. They are not even considered at all. They are nothing; they don't count; they don't matter. They are commodities like TV sets and cell phones. We have actually turned animals into inanimate objects – sandwiches and shoes.*"

GARY YOUROFSKY

"*The following is a rap I wrote as a tribute to Gary Yourofsky and his iconic, passionate, and provocative vegan speech – a speech that went viral and was translated into 30 languages. (You can find it on my website at vivianchinelli.com.)*"

VIVIAN CHINELLI

HE'LL NEVER STOP

He is an activist and educator filled with compassion, with a passion for justice that isn't yet in fashion. An animal lover who's fought for animals that we forgot, and he'll never stop. I'll never stop.

He freed the minks from a farm where the farmers bore arms to slaughter all the animals and cause them great harm. Against some advice, for saving animals' lives, he paid the price, got arrested, then they banished him twice.

The UK and Canada, they don't want him either. He's a leader, not a meat eater, beater or cheater. Connection and protection. He's spreading the news, so that we can have the information from which to choose.

And now it's time for introductions. Gary will speak. Here's a spoiler alert, or a sneak peek, he isn't meek. Hate or adore, Gary might make you sore, but he will rock you to the core and have you begging for more.

"Hello, I'm Gary Yourofsky and I'm not here to change you, rearrange you, take your religion or estrange you. You can keep your politics, social media clicks, get your Breaking News fix, and keep on doing all your old tricks.

Listen to Ted Nugent if you really like his voice. My intention's not to take away, or make you change your voice choice. Just wanna connect you to the person that you once were, loving scales and feathers and the animals with fur, sir.

I'm here to challenge your beliefs. I'll be intense, get you off the fence. Put in my two cents. Love and empathy are my defense. Do unto others. They're our sisters and brothers. They have families like us and they are fathers and mothers. →

vivianchinelli.com

"Everyone thinks of changing the world, but no one thinks of changing himself."

LEO TOLSTOY

I'M NOT VEGAN BUT MY COUSIN IS

Mistreat them then we eat them all without a grain of blame, shame! Open your eyes to the bullshit and the lies game. Names like beef and bacon in an effort to disguise, guys. They cry out in pain, in vain. It's insane!

Non-fiction, meat addiction, domination these are more words. It's a grave abomination moving backwards and not forwards. The most important four words, but sadly most ignored words, 'Thou Shall Not Kill.'

Watch some footage, you'll be shocked, confused and conflicted. You'll see pain you pay for and just how it's inflicted. Don't turn away. Do more than pray for the animals we brutalize, day after each and every day.

We pick and choose who to brutalize and then decide to slaughter. You won't show those graphic photos to your son or to your daughter 'cause they'll look you in the eye and cry. Then ask you why … why that precious pig or calf or chick had to die.

My speech is almost over now. My plan was to inspire. Require you to think and raise your consciousness higher. I hope that in your belly is desire on fire, so now what are you going to do?"

It's on you.

vivianchinelli.com

"I've always abhorred violence and am highly sensitized to it. I do not think it benefits society or indeed any individual to become tolerant of violence. I feel if I can accept the abuse of these innocent, sentient creatures and my role in it then I could easily become apathetic about ... well, everything, and that is a scary thought."

EVANNA LYNCH

BUT WHERE DO I START?

*"I wanna be vegan just like you.
But where do I start and what do I do?"*

You start by giving yourself a hand
for thinking of doing a thing this grand!

Then talk to someone
with whom you connect,
a vegan whose opinion
you fully respect.
If you don't know a vegan,
then get online.
Read and watch what you can.
You're gonna be fine!

Meet vegans in meetups.
Join a challenge or two.
There are vegans on social media,
much more than a few
who will happily guide you
through this awesome task.
If you find you have questions,
be bold and just ask.

Your journey has started.
Be excited. (You're allowed!)
It's a road worth traveling.
It's a great choice. Be proud!

vivianchinelli.com

"If you think you can't go vegan overnight, make a plan. For instance, you can start by eliminating all products made from pigs. Once you see how easy it is, pick another animal. Then another. This strategy has worked for so many people. Maybe it will work for you, too.

Or just try eating plant-based today. Then try it tomorrow. Then the next day. Take it one day at a time, and in time, you might be surprised that leaving animal products off your plate was easier than you thought.

In the meantime, you can start by not supporting businesses that exploit and abuse animals for clothing, accessories, personal care products and entertainment. I know you can do it and I'm confident that you will feel empowered when you do!"

VIVIAN CHINELLI

THE LEAP

They took the leap.
It wasn't steep. It was flat.
And they became vegan, just like that.

Some things you know in your heart that they're right,
so it's easy to make such a leap overnight.

Some folks can change their course on a dime,
but if that isn't you, go ahead, take some time.

No matter how you do it, please don't wait forever.
Do the research, plan your strategies,
be thoughtful and clever.
It's a worthy endeavor.
So never say never.

And you, too, will take the leap one day.

vivianchinelli.com

"If a kid ever realized what was involved in factory farming, they would never touch meat again."

JAMES CROMWELL

"I have a dream that all animals on Earth will have peace in their lives. We all deserve it, human or not. For this, I have fought. It's just that simple: Don't eat meat. This is my vegan dream."

GENESIS BUTLER

CARTOON ANIMALS

Hello little girl and hello little boy.
I know we cartoon animals appear so full of joy.

But, smiling pigs are what they show you.
What the truth is, you don't know.
You're always taught that we are happy.

And the lie just goes on.

Cheerful cows? What is hidden?
Things folks do that are *not* forbidden, like
stealing my baby on the day that she's born.

They just keep piling it on.

We, chickens, gladly offering eggs
while wobbling on our broken legs?
And you're made to think we feel no pain.

It's all one big con.

Remembering commercials that were on T.V.,
like cartoon Charlie from the sea –
a tuna begging, "Please, take me!"

Keeps that lie going strong.

One day when you have gotten older,
feeling smarter and much bolder,
you will seek out what the truth is,
so the lie *cannot* go on … anymore!

vivianchinelli.com

> "*It's pretty amazing to wake up every morning, knowing that every decision I make is to cause as little harm as possible. It's a pretty fantastic way to live.*"
>
> COLLEEN PATRICK-GOUDREAU

LIVING IN PEACE

Monkeys, pigs, dogs.
Chickens, cats, frogs.
Lambs, turkeys, hogs.
Can't we get along?

Elephants and whales.
Crocodiles and snails.
Cows and bears and quails.
Where did we go wrong?

I had hoped we were "*all for one*,"
instead of "*us*" and "*oh, they're just the others.*"

Imagine if we all lived together in peace
and behaved as loving sisters and brothers!

"No human influenced me to become vegan. The screaming, terrified, enslaved animals were the only influence needed."

GARY YOUROFSKY

YEH, BUT ...

Did you know that by choosing to eat animals we are paying for their abuse?

Yeh, but ... animals are here for us.
Yeh, but ... we've always eaten animals.
Yeh, but ... going vegan is expensive.
Yeh, but ... what about farmers' jobs?
Yeh, but ... eating animals is part of the "Circle of Life."
Yeh, but ... we have canine teeth.
Yeh, but ... everything in moderation.
Yeh, but ... morality is subjective.
Yeh, but ... let's just improve their conditions.
Yeh, but ... plants feel pain, too.
Yeh, but ... it's all part of the food chain.
Yeh, but ... what about human rights issues?
Yeh, but ... eating animals is so convenient.
Yeh, but ... predators eat their prey.
Yeh, but ... one person can't make a difference.
Yeh, but ... eating meat is cultural, traditional and legal.
Yeh, but ... eating animals is my personal choice.
Yeh, but ... if I go vegan, my family won't understand.
Yeh, but ... God says that I should eat animals.
Yeh, but ... I need my animal protein.
Yeh, but ... I love how animals taste.
Yeh, but ... I'm too old to change.

To hear respectful rebuttals for these "Yeh, buts," search "Earthling Ed's 30 Excuses."
He'll challenge your thinking and make you think twice about paying for all the abuses.

vivianchinelli.com

"At some point, you have to decide who you are and what matters morally to you. And once you decide that you regard victimizing vulnerable nonhumans is not morally acceptable, it is easy to go and stay vegan."

GARY L. FRANCIONE

THE DECISION

Some people re-decide, every day,
about a thing they've already decided.

It's hard to move forward with confidence,
if you always stay halfway divided.

Once you've decided that cruelty is wrong,
deciding yet again makes the process too long.

So, decide to move forward and always stay strong.
And decide on the side of compassion.

vivianchinelli.com

"*Never believe that a few caring people can't change the world. For, indeed, that's all who ever have.*"

MARGARET MEAD

THE RIPPLE EFFECT

Each little ripple in the sea
can change the tide for you and me.

So be that ripple and start a new trend.
Change the world with your actions.
Be vegan, my friend.

"Believe in yourself! Have faith in your abilities! Without a humble but reasonable confidence in your own powers you cannot be successful or happy."

NORMAN VINCENT PEALE

YOU CAN DO IT!

Thinking of going vegan?

You can *do it*!
You can *do it*!
You can *do it*!

You can *do it*!
You can *do it*!

You can *do it*!
If you put your mind to it!

No, really! You ***CAN*** do it!

And you'll feel so empowered when you do!

vivianchinelli.com

> "Going vegan is not the most you can do. It's the least you can do."

> NATASHA KATHERINE CUCULOVSKI AND LUCA PADALINI

> "Our lives begin to end the day we become silent about things that matter."

> MARTIN LUTHER KING, JR.,

SPREADING THE WORD

They say going vegan's the least you can do.
So, get out now and go spread the word.
Please engage in respectful dialogue.
Just make sure that our message is heard.

You can wow some folks on the internet
with a yummy plant-based recipe.
You can TikTok and Zoom it,
but please don't assume
it will happen without you and me.

Talk to strangers on the street.
Hold up signs. March with others.
Send a petition to a politician, or call.
Any act that you do to forward the cause
will never be considered "small."

Write a book. Write a song.
Do what's right. Right a wrong.
Things will change.
Just wait and you'll see.

Write a blog or a rhyme.
Don't give up.
Trust in time that
the animals we fight for ...
will be free!

vivianchinelli.com

"Becoming a vegan is not about self-denial; it's more a matter of self-awareness. It is about trying new foods and broadening your palate, expressing the joy of being alive, and knowing that you're making a daily effort to live less violently and more sustainably."

GENE BAUR

THESE VEGANS

Fathers and mothers, sisters and brothers,
basketball players, mayors and others.
Stylists and pilots, doctors and dentists,
folks who paint houses and those who mend fences.

Tailors and sailors and so many teachers,
nurses and skateboarders, gardeners and preachers.
Cousins and dog walkers, actors, professors,
cleaners and clerks and movie set dressers.

Retirees, artists and drivers and cooks,
bosses and assistants and those who love books.
Students and friends who play the kazoo (I do),
and millions of people ... just like you!

When you ask these vegans,
"What's your biggest regret?"
This is the answer they'll give you, I bet.

"I wish I had become vegan sooner."

But there's no going back.
We must start where we are.
So choose now to be vegan.
It will be one of your best choices,
BY FAR.

vivianchinelli.com

Dear Readers,

This may be the end of my rhymes and raps,
but it's hardly the end.

Visit me at vivianchinelli.com for more good stuff
about respecting and protecting animals,
our health and our planet.

Let's stay connected and change the world together!

ACKNOWLEDGEMENTS

I have so many fabulous folks to thank for helping me create "I'M NOT VEGAN BUT MY COUSIN IS."

First, I'd like to express my utmost gratitude to three special people without whom I never would have written this book—Hanna Golan, Suzanna McGee, and Rick Chinelli.

To Hanna, my first and dear vegan friend, thank you for continuing to love me during all those years when I chose not to face the harsh reality of animal exploitation. Your steady persistence and utmost patience helped me finally walk my talk and become the person I always wanted to be. I also want to thank you, Halinka, for reading and polishing my work and for being a thoughtful vegan advisor. Your dedication to helping me streamline my thoughts inspired me to improve my writing.

To Suzanna, my clever friend and coach, I am so grateful that you pushed me (oops, I mean, encouraged me) not only to write this book but also to create a companion website on which to share other good stuff. Excellent thinking, Suzanna (as always)! You never miss an opportunity to expand my horizons. Your clever ideas (technical and editorial) were incredibly invaluable and spot-on.

To Rick, my beloved husband, thank you for 40 years of unwavering love and encouragement. You helped me with some pretty wild and crazy projects during my teaching years, and here you are again, doing the same. Thank you for all your creative suggestions and hands-on technical support. I couldn't have done it without you. You rock, Chinelli!

To all the amazing people whose quotations I have included in my book, I am honored and very grateful to be able to share your passionate, thoughtful, and powerful words with my readers.

vivianchinelli.com

To Amy Lacombe, Eve Rosenberg, and Elly Fry – thank you, from the bottom of my heart, for graciously agreeing to read through each of my rhymes with a fine-toothed comb and for advising me, as needed. Gals, I can't tell you how much it meant to me for you to invest that kind of time and love into my project.

Shellby Benefield and Ellyn Weiss, thank you so much for reciting my rhymes out loud so that I could hear what they sound like when someone other than I was reading them. Ladies, your interpretations of my rhythmic stories were music to my ears.

I am very grateful to Diane Rose-Solomon for recommending I use Pedernales Publishing to help me self-publish my book. It was a pleasure working with Jose Ramirez and his team. We worked closely to create an inviting and professional-looking finished product. Many thanks, José.

I tip my hat to Kim Delgado for connecting me with activists whose vision I share. And to Sarah Segal for, among other things, introducing me to my favorite holiday word, "Thanks*Living*."

I am much obliged to Allison Thomas, Courtney Simpson, Kara Mondino, Keia Black, Madison Tully, Patricia Mace, and Samantha Steindel-Cymer for helping me clarify my vegan message. Thank you, ladies, for your thoughtful edits and valuable input.

To my friends, family, and strangers, thank you for allowing me to engage you in a dialogue about veganism. Your questions, comments, and concerns inspired so many of my rhymes.

I am grateful to the hundreds of resources (activists, websites, recipes, speeches, documentaries, conversations, and the like) that laid the foundation for my vegan education. A special shoutout goes to the websites where I found most of the quotes that I cite in the book.

To friends and family members who kept asking me how my book was coming along, let me just say that your encouragement meant a lot to me. Thank you.

Last, but not least, I would like to address my fellow Vegan Toastmasters (at Toastmasters International). Spending time with passionate animal defenders like you is akin to enjoying the cherry on top of an already delicious vegan chocolate sundae. Your astute guidance has given me confidence to speak cogently and vociferously for the animals.

NOTE: If you are vegan, pre-vegan, vegan-curious, a plant-based eater, or just someone who would like to improve your public speaking skills, please join us on the internet at vegan.toastmastersclubs.org. We would love to have you visit one of our meetings!

vivianchinelli.com

APPENDIX
QUOTATION CONTRIBUTORS AND CREDITS

I hope that the quotations I selected for my book were as meaningful to you as they are to me. If so, I strongly encourage you to search the internet for their authors. While it is impossible to list all the authors' accomplishments here, many have created organizations and websites, written books, or have a social media presence that can provide you with continued inspiration.

I am extremely grateful to all of the contributors! I would also like to thank activists Gary Yourofsky and Ed Winters (Earthling Ed) whose names I used in a couple of my rhymes.

LIFE'S CHOICES
- MISCHA TEMAUL, AUTHOR
- PYTHAGORAS, PHILOSOPHER

INSPIRED
- EVE ROSENBERG, AUTHOR
- ANGELA DAVIS, POLITICAL ACTIVIST, AUTHOR

INVISIBLE FORCE
- MELANIE JOY, AUTHOR OF "WHY WE LOVE DOGS, EAT PIGS, AND WEAR COWS: AN INTRODUCTION TO CARNISM"
- JO-ANNE MCARTHUR, PHOTOJOURNALIST, FOUNDER OF WE ANIMALS MEDIA
- ALEX O'CONNOR (Cosmic Skeptic), PHILOSOPHER

WHAT ABOUT PROTEIN?
- T. COLIN CAMPBELL, NUTRITIONAL BIOCHEMIST, AUTHOR OF THE CHINA STUDY: REVISED AND EXPANDED EDITION: THE MOST COMPREHENSIVE STUDY OF NUTRITION EVER CONDUCTED AND THE STARTLING IMPLICATIONS FOR DIET, WEIGHT LOSS AND LONG-TERM HEALTH"
- CARL LEWIS, ATHLETE

DO UNTO MOTHERS
- PETER SINGER, AUTHOR OF "ANIMAL LIBERATION"
- DR. MILTON MILLS, MD, PLANT-BASED PHYSICIAN
- VIVIAN CHINELLI, AUTHOR OF "I'M NOT VEGAN BUT MY COUSIN IS: RHYMES, RAPS AND OTHER GOOD STUFF ABOUT RESPECTING AND PROTECTING ANIMALS, OUR HEALTH AND OUR PLANET"

ONE, TWO, BUCKLE MY SHOE
- INGRID NEWKIRK, PRESIDENT OF PEOPLE FOR THE ETHICAL TREATMENT OF ANIMALS (PETA)

DOWNSTREAM
- POPE JOHN PAUL II
- NATIVE AMERICAN PROVERB

MANURE
- BARBARA WARD, SOCIAL ANTHROPOLOGIST
- JAMES CAMERON, FILMMAKER, EXECUTIVE PRODUCER OF THE DOCUMENTARY "THE GAME CHANGERS"

I'M NOT VEGAN BUT MY COUSIN IS
- GRETA THUNBERG, CLIMATE ACTIVIST (INSPIRED YOUTH CLIMATE MOVEMENT)

YOUR TURN
- THE BUDDHA DHAMMAPADA
- JEREMY BENTHAM, PHILOSOPHER, SOCIAL REFORMER

IF YOU KNEW
- DR. JANE GOODALL, DBE FOUNDER OF THE JANE GOODALL INSTITUTE, U.N. MESSENGER OF PEACE

BYE-BYE, RAINFOREST
- VINITA KINRA, AUTHOR
- FRANKLIN D. ROOSEVELT, 32ND PRESIDENT OF THE UNITED STATES OF AMERICA

GASSY
- VEGA THE COW AT CLIMATEHEALERS.ORG

A WARNING FROM YOUR "MEAT"
- CENTER FOR DISEASE CONTROL AND PREVENTION, ARTICLE "ZOONOTIC DISEASES"

HEALTH INTERTWINED
- GRETA THUNBERG, YOUTH CLIMATE ACTIVIST (INSPIRED YOUTH CLIMATE MOVEMENT)
- JOHN ROBBINS, AUTHOR OF "DIET FOR A NEW AMERICA"

HUMANKIND
- RALPH WALDO EMERSON, ESSAYIST
- JOAQUIN PHOENIX, ACTOR
- ABRAHAM LINCOLN, 16TH PRESIDENT OF THE UNITED STATES OF AMERICA

SLAM, BAM
- HOPE FERDOWSIAN, MD, AUTHOR OF "PHOENIX ZONES: WHERE STRENGTH IS BORN AND RESILIENCE LIVES"
- JAMES ASPEY, ANIMAL RIGHTS ACTIVIST

DON'T SELL YOURSELF SHORT
- RALPH WALDO EMERSON, ESSAYIST
- SHAUN MONSON, FILMMAKER, DIRECTOR OF THE DOCUMENTARIES "DOMINION" AND "EARTHLINGS"

GOOD GRIEF!
- CAPTAIN PAUL WATSON, FOUNDER OF SEA SHEPHERD CONSERVATION SOCIETY

DO UNTO FISH
- "MEAT YOUR FUTURE" WEBSITE
- FRANZ KAFKA, NOVELIST (WHILE ADMIRING FISH IN AN AQUARIUM)

DUPED NO MORE
- MAYA ANGELOU, POET, CIVIL RIGHTS ACTIVIST
- ALBERT EINSTEIN, PHYSICIST

DEFINITELY NO!
- LYRICS FROM THE ROGERS AND HAMMERSTEIN'S SONG BY THAT NAME.
- DR. MILTON MILLS, MD, PLANT-BASED PHYSICIAN

DO THE MATH
- VIVIAN CHINELLI, AUTHOR OF "I'M NOT VEGAN BUT MY COUSIN IS: RHYMES, RAPS AND OTHER GOOD STUFF ABOUT RESPECTING AND PROTECTING ANIMALS, OUR HEALTH AND OUR PLANET"

IT'S A THING
- VIVIAN CHINELLI, AUTHOR OF "I'M NOT VEGAN BUT MY COUSIN IS: RHYMES, RAPS AND OTHER GOOD STUFF ABOUT RESPECTING AND PROTECTING ANIMALS, OUR HEALTH AND OUR PLANET"
- JASMINE C. LEYVA, DIRECTOR OF THE DOCUMENTARY "THE INVISIBLE VEGAN"

FEEDING THE HUNGRY
- PHILIP WOLLEN, FOUNDER OF WINDSOME CONSTANCE KINDNESS
- MICHELLE OBAMA, FIRST LADY OF THE UNITED STATES OF AMERICA

DO UNTO PIGLETS
- RYAN GOSLING, ACTOR
- SIR PAUL MCCARTNEY, MEMBER OF THE BEATLES, SINGER, SONGWRITER

SCARED
- ANTHONY DOUGLAS WILLIAMS, AUTHOR
- LEO TOLSTOY, AUTHOR
- MARTIN BUBER, PHILOSOPHER

PROCRASTINATED
- SUZY AMIS CAMERON, ENVIRONMENTAL ADVOCATE
- GARY L. FRANCIONE, PROFESSOR, ANIMAL RIGHTS PHILOSOPHER

THE NEW TALK
- PLUTARCH, PHILOSOPHER
- LEONARDO DA VINCI, POLYMATH
- ALBERT EINSTEIN, PHYSICIST

YOUNG DAD GOES VEGAN
- THE GOLDEN RULE (IT CAN BE FOUND IN SOME FORM IN ALMOST EVERY ETHICAL TRADITION)
- W.E.B. DU BOIS, SOCIOLOGIST, CIVIL RIGHTS ACTIVIST

FEEDING OUR CHILDREN
- MAYIM BIALEK, ACTRESS
- AKBARALI JETHA, AUTHOR

COGNITIVE DISSONANCE
- EVE ROSENBERG, AUTHOR

STREET CONVERSATION
- ONE OF THE TRANSLATIONS OF GENESIS 1:29
- ANTHONY DOUGLAS WILLIAMS, AUTHOR

GOD'S FIRST CHOICE
- JACQUES DEVAL, PLAYWRIGHT
- UNKNOWN

WHAT ABOUT HONEY?
- VIVIAN CHINELLI, AUTHOR OF "I'M NOT VEGAN BUT MY COUSIN IS: RHYMES, RAPS AND OTHER GOOD STUFF ABOUT RESPECTING, PROTECTING ANIMALS, OUR HEALTH AND OUR PLANET"

FOIE GRAS (fwäh gräh)
- CASEY AFFLECK, ACTOR

IN A VEGAN WORLD
- JACO VAN DRONGELEN
- VIVIAN CHINELLI, AUTHOR OF "I'M NOT VEGAN BUT MY COUSIN IS: RHYMES, RAPS AND OTHER GOOD STUFF ABOUT RESPECTING AND PROTECTING ANIMALS, OUR HEALTH AND OUR PLANET"

IN MODERATION
- COLLEEN PATRICK-GOUDREAU, AUTHOR OF "THE JOYFUL VEGAN"

OUR CHOICE
- MOBY, SINGER, SONGWRITER
- DAVID HAYE, HEAVY WEIGHT BOXER, TWO-TIME WORLD CHAMPION

LITTLE MISS MUFFET
- BETH ARNOLD, AUTHOR OF "ALWAYS BE KIND"
- JOAQUIN PHOENIX, ACTOR
- VIVIAN CHINELLI, AUTHOR OF "I'M NOT VEGAN BUT MY COUSIN IS: RHYMES, RAPS AND OTHER GOOD STUFF ABOUT RESPECTING AND PROTECTING ANIMALS, OUR HEALTH AND OUR PLANET"

vivianchinelli.com

A VEGAN TWIST
- DR. CALDWELL ESSELSTYN, MD, AUTHOR OF "PREVENT AND REVERSE HEART DISEASE"
- BARBARA THOMPSON, COMMUNITY ACTIVIST
- TABITHA BROWN, VEGAN SOCIAL MEDIA INFLUENCER, ACTRESS, AUTHOR

TURKEY TALK
- DEXTER SCOTT KING, CIVIL RIGHTS ACTIVIST, AUTHOR
- BILLIE EILISH, SINGER, SONGWRITER

ALONE
- VIVIAN CHINELLI, AUTHOR OF "I'M NOT VEGAN BUT MY COUSIN IS: RHYMES, RAPS AND OTHER GOOD STUFF ABOUT RESPECTING AND PROTECTING ANIMALS, OUR HEALTH AND OUR PLANET"

DO UNTO CHICKENS
- ZOE WEIL, CO-FOUNDER AND PRESIDENT OF THE INSTITUTE FOR HUMANE EDUCATION
- DAVID ATTENBOROUGH, NATURAL HISTORIAN AND AUTHOR
- JOEY CARBSTRONG, ANIMAL RIGHTS ACTIVIST

WHAT'S THE DEAL?
- RUSSELL BRAND, ACTOR
- ALICE WALKER, CIVIL RIGHTS ACTIVIST, FIRST AFRICAN-AMERICAN WOMAN TO WIN A PULITZER PRIZE FOR LITERATURE

CIRCLE OF COMPASSION
- ALBERT SCHWEITZER, HUMANITARIAN, PHILOSOPHER, PHYSICIAN
- THICH NHAT HANH, BUDDHIST TEACHER, PEACE ACTIVIST

LISTEN UP
- SIMONE REYES, ANIMAL ACTIVIST
- ALICIA SILVERSTONE, ACTRESS

BEST FRIENDS
- INGRID NEWKIRK, PRESIDENT OF PEOPLE FOR THE ETHICAL TREATMENT OF ANIMALS (PETA)
- THOMAS EDISON, INVENTOR

INTERVIEW WITH FACTORY FARMED ANIMALS
- PETER SINGER, AUTHOR OF "ANIMAL LIBERATION"
- EMILY MORAN BARWICK, ANIMAL RIGHTS ACTIVIST AND EDUCATOR

IN SHORT
- MAHATMA GANDHI, PHILOSOPHER OF NON-VIOLENCE

AG-GAG
- JAMES WILDMAN, M. ED, HUMANE EDUCATOR FOR THE ANIMAL RIGHTS FOUNDATION OF FLORIDA

PLACES
- GENE BAUR, AUTHOR OF "FARM SANCTUARY: CHANGING HEARTS AND MINDS ABOUT ANIMALS AND FOOD"
- ALEX HERSHAFT, HOLOCAUST SURVIVOR, CO-FOUNDER OF THE FARM ANIMAL RIGHTS MOVEMENT

HAPPY ANIMALS
- JENNY BROWN, AUTHOR OF "THE LUCKY ONES: MY PASSIONATE FIGHT FOR FARM ANIMALS"
- VIVIAN CHINELLI, AUTHOR OF "I'M NOT VEGAN BUT MY COUSIN IS: RHYMES, RAPS AND OTHER GOOD STUFF ABOUT RESPECTING AND PROTECTING ANIMALS, OUR HEALTH AND OUR PLANET"

HEY DIDDLE DIDDLE
- JOEY CARBSTRONG, ANIMAL RIGHTS ACTIVIST

A FIVE-YEAR-OLD SPEAKS
- VIVIAN CHINELLI, AUTHOR OF "I'M NOT VEGAN BUT MY COUSIN IS: RHYMES, RAPS AND OTHER GOOD STUFF ABOUT RESPECTING AND PROTECTING ANIMALS, OUR HEALTH AND OUR PLANET"
- BARACK OBAMA, 44TH PRESIDENT OF THE UNITED STATES OF AMERICA

MARY HAD A LITTLE LAMB
- GEORGE BERNARD SHAW, PLAYWRIGHT

BUT I'M VEGETARIAN ALREADY
- RAI AREN, AUTHOR

BOYCOTT
- CESAR CHAVEZ, COMMUNITY ORGANIZER, CIVIL RIGHTS ACTIVIST
- STACEYANN CHIN, POET, POLITICAL ACTIVIST
- DOLORES HUERTA, COMMUNITY ORGANIZER, CIVIL RIGHTS ACTIVIST

TO EAT OR NOT TO EAT
- GEORGE BERNARD SHAW, PLAYWRIGHT
- LEONARDO DI VINCI, POLYMATH

A FISH SPEAKS
- ALBERT EINSTEIN, PHYSICIST
- SHRIMAD BHAGAVAD GITA (HINDU SCRIPTURE)

CATCH AND RELEASE
- JOSEPH WOOD KRUTCH, WRITER, NATURALIST

VEGAN RESTAURANTS
- LED, OWNER OF GREEN TABLE CAFÉ, LOS ANGELES
- ERYKAH BADU, SINGER, SONGWRITER

vivianchinelli.com

PARAKEET PETER
- PAUL LAURENCE DUNBAR, POET, SON OF SLAVES
- TENNESSEE WILLIAMS, PLAYWRIGHT

ANIMAL DOCS
- LOUIS J. CAMUTI, VETERINARIAN
- VIVIAN CHINELLI, AUTHOR OF "I'M NOT VEGAN BUT MY COUSIN IS: RHYMES, RAPS AND OTHER GOOD STUFF ABOUT RESPECTING AND PROTECTING ANIMALS, OUR HEALTH AND OUR PLANET"

TESTING 1, 2, 3
- CHARLES MAGEL, PHILOSOPHER

THE LEAPING BUNNY SPEAKS
- BLUE CROSS OF INDIA FACEBOOK PAGE

GET ON BOARD
- VICTORIA MORAN, AUTHOR OF "MAIN STREET VEGAN"

BORN TO BE ME
- MARY TYLER MOORE, ACTRESS
- GLENDA JACKSON, ACTRESS

BAD BEHAVIOR
- GARY FRANCIONE, PROFESSOR, ANIMAL RIGHTS PHILOSOPHER
- JANE VELEZ-MITCHELL, TV AND SOCIAL MEDIA JOURNALIST, FOUNDER OF UNCHAINEDTV.COM

READY, AIM, TAKE A LIFE
- JIMMY STEWART, ACTOR

HE'LL NEVER STOP
- GARY YOUROFSKY, ANIMAL RIGHTS ACTIVIST AND EDUCATOR
- VIVIAN CHINELLI, AUTHOR OF "I'M NOT VEGAN BUT MY COUSIN IS: RHYMES, RAPS AND OTHER GOOD STUFF ABOUT RESPECTING AND PROTECTING ANIMALS, OUR HEALTH AND OUR PLANET"

- LEO TOLSTOY, AUTHOR

BUT WHERE DO I START?
- EVANNA LYNCH, ACTRESS, AUTHOR

THE LEAP
- VIVIAN CHINELLI, AUTHOR OF "I'M NOT VEGAN BUT MY COUSIN IS: RHYMES, RAPS AND OTHER GOOD STUFF ABOUT RESPECTING AND PROTECTING ANIMALS, OUR HEALTH AND OUR PLANET"

CARTOON ANIMALS
- JAMES CROMWELL, ACTOR
- GENESIS BUTLER, TEEN ACTIVIST

LIVING IN PEACE
- COLLEEN PATRICK-GOUDREAU, AUTHOR OF "THE JOYFUL VEGAN"

YEH, BUT ...
- GARY YOUROFSKY, ANIMAL RIGHTS ACTIVIST AND EDUCATOR

THE DECISION
- GARY L. FRANCIONE, PROFESSOR, ANIMAL RIGHTS PHILOSOPHER

THE RIPPLE EFFECT
- MARGARET MEAD, CULTURAL ANTHROPOLOGIST

YOU CAN DO IT!
- NORMAN VINCENT PEALE, AUTHOR

SPREADING THE WORD
- NATASHA KATHERINE CUCULOVSKI AND LUCA PADALINI, VEGAN EDUCATORS KNOWN AS "THAT VEGAN COUPLE"
- MARTIN LUTHER KING, JR., CIVIL RIGHTS ACTIVIST

THESE VEGANS
- GENE BAUR, AUTHOR OF "FARM SANCTUARY: CHANGING HEARTS AND MINDS ABOUT ANIMALS AND FOOD"

vivianchinelli.com